# CAN DO
## Cool Creations

## Books in the series:

 **Familiar Things**
by Sally Thomas

 **Eco-Ventures**
by Hannah Sugar, Kids' Clubs Network

 **Serious Fun: Games for 4–9s**
by Phill Burton, Dynamix

 **Whatever the Weather**
by Jane Gallagher

 **Cool Creations**
by Mary Allanson, Kids' Clubs Network

 **Serious Fun: Games for 10–14s**
by Phill Burton, Dynamix

 **Sticks and Stones**
by Sharon Crockett

## Series Foreword

Children and young people of all ages should be able to initiate and develop their own play. Adult involvement should be based on careful observation, appropriate consultation and response to what the children need in terms of their development at this time and in this place.

Play is freely chosen personally directed behaviour motivated from within. Adults can create the best possible conditions for play: the time, space, materials, safety and support for children to develop the skills and understanding they need to extend the possibilities of their play. The degree to which the children and young people are able to make any activity their own will determine its success as a play opportunity rather than simply 'entertainment', a means of 'keeping them busy' or producing 'something to take home to parents'.

Many of the ideas in these books are not new. Indeed play games and creative activities are passed on across many generations and between different cultures across the world, constantly being adapted and changed to suit a new time, a new group of children, a new environment.

We have acknowledged sources and sought permission wherever it has been possible to do so. We hope, and indeed anticipate, that the ideas in these books will be adapted and developed further by those that use them and would be very interested to hear your comments, thoughts, ideas and suggestions.
www.thomsonlearning.co.uk/childcare

Annie Davy

# CAN DO
## Cool Creations

By Mary Allanson

Series Editor: Annie Davy

KIDS' CLUBS NETWORK

**THOMSON**

Australia • Canada • Mexico • Singapore • Spain • United Kingdom • United States

Cool Creations

Copyright © Kids' Clubs Network 2002

The Thomson logo is a registered trademark used herein under licence.

For more information, contact Thomson, High Holborn House, 50–51 Bedford Row, London, WC1R 4LR or visit us on the World Wide Web at: http://www.thomsonlearning.co.uk

All rights reserved by Thomson 2002. The text of this publication, or any part thereof, may not be reproduced or transmitted in any form or by any means, electronic or mechanical, including photocopying, recording, storage in an information retrieval system, or otherwise, without prior permission of the publisher.

While the publisher has taken all reasonable care in the preparation of this book the publisher makes no representation, express or implied, with regard to the accuracy of the information contained in this book and cannot accept any legal responsibility or liability for any errors or omissions from the book or the consequences thereof.

Products and services that are referred to in this book may be either trademarks and/or registered trademarks of their respective owners. The publisher and author/s make no claim to these trademarks.

British Library Cataloguing-in-Publication Data
A catalogue record for this book is available from the British Library

ISBN 1-86152-967-8

First edition 2002

Typeset by Bottle & Co., Banbury, UK

Printed in Croatia by Zrinski

Text design by Bottle & Co.

COOL CREATIONS

# Contents

**Series Introduction** vi–vii

**Introduction** viii

**Acknowledgements** viii

### Funky Fashion
| | |
|---|---|
| Fabric Painting | 1 |
| Friendship Bracelets & Hair Braiding | 4 |
| Making faces | 7 |
| Putting on the Style | 10 |

### Media Madness
| | |
|---|---|
| Fun with Photos | 13 |
| Newspaper Know-How | 16 |
| Roving Reporters | 19 |
| Video Ventures | 22 |

### Changing Rooms
| | |
|---|---|
| Wicked Walls | 25 |
| New for Old | 28 |
| Dough Designs | 31 |
| Comfy Cushions | 34 |

### Let's Get Physical
| | |
|---|---|
| Kick Rounders | 37 |
| Crossfire | 40 |
| Defender | 42 |
| Dodgeball Activities—3 Games | 44 |

### Munch Bunch
| | |
|---|---|
| Breakfast Club | 47 |
| Mega Meals—Volcanic Chilli Con Carne | 51 |
| Cool Cocktails | 55 |
| Snack Attack | 58 |
| Party Pieces | 61 |

### Circus Skills
| | |
|---|---|
| Great Balls of Beans | 64 |
| Whats Round Goes Round | 67 |
| Walk Tall—Making Stilts | 70 |
| Stilt Walking | 73 |
| The Final Curtain | 75 |

CAN DO

# Series Introduction

The CAN DO series is an intensely practical resource for children who attend childcare settings, drop in centres or playsettings out of school, and for those of you who work with them in these settings. Anyone working with children, whether as a trainee, an experienced manager or as a volunteer will sometimes get tired, feel jaded or simply seek new inspiration. Whether you are a childminder, a playworker, a family centre worker or a day nursery assistant or manager, you will find a rich source of ideas for children of all ages in the CAN DO series. In these books you will find practical answers to the difficult 'CAN DO' questions which are often asked of adults working with children:

- Child coming in from school, 'What can I do today?'
- Parent visiting a childminder: 'What exactly can the children do here?'
- Playworker or Childcare worker at a team meeting: 'What can we do to extend the range of play provision here?'

The series is structured towards 3 different age ranges— 0–3, 4–9 and 10–14, but many of the books will be used successfully by or with older or younger children. The books are written by authors with a wide range of experience in working with children and young people, and who have a thorough understanding of the value of play and the possibilities and constraints of work in childcare and play settings.

COOL CREATIONS

Each activity is introduced with a 'why we like it' section, which explains why children and adults who work with children have found this to be something that they enjoyed, or that has enhanced their play provision. Many of the activities also have 'Snapshots' and 'Spotlight' boxes which expand on the possibilities as developed by children, or an approach you can take in working with children. These sections are intended to help you reflect on your work and the quality of what is provided.

The ideas in this series are intended to be playful, inclusive and affordable. They are not based on any prescribed curriculum, but they could be used to enrich and develop almost any setting in which children play and learn. They do not rely on expensive toys and equipment; they are environmentally friendly and are peppered with practical tips and health and safety checkpoints.

## Language used in the book

YOU (the reader): The books are addressed to children and the adults who work with them together. Older children will be able to use the books themselves or with a little co-operation from adults. There are some activities where adult supervision or assistance will be required (in developing and supervising safe working with tools for example) and this is highlighted where relevant.

**SETTING:** We have used the term 'setting' rather than club, scheme, centre, etc. as the generic term to describe the range of contexts for childcare and playwork including childminders' homes. The 'Snapshots' draw on a range of different settings to illustrate the development of some of the activities in practice.

**PLAYLEADER:** This term is predominantly used in the 4–9 and 10–14 series, as this is the most familiar generic term that covers adults working with these age groups in out of school settings.

# Cool Creations

## Introduction

When a group were asked what they wanted to do out of school hours they said, 'We want our time to be structured but we don't want to be too organised. We want workers who are available but who don't interfere. We want our own base but we also want lots of trips out. We want premises that are bright and airy but when given a choice we may decide we prefer a basement . We want to feel safe but we also want excitement. We want an area where we can sit and relax with friends, where we can read magazines or listen to music and we want somewhere to make drinks and snacks. We want lots of activities going on, but participation has to be voluntary and we also want plenty of free time.'

The selection of activities in this book has been chosen to reflect the diverse and often contradictory needs of the 10–14 year age group. It is not intended to be definitive but to provide starting points for creative, fertile minds to develop and expand. Most of the activities form a framework on which to build according to the interest, imagination and ability of those taking part.

**Mary Allanson**
Kids' Clubs Network

## Acknowledgements for *Cool Creations*

THANKS GO TO COLLEAGUES AT KIDS' CLUBS NETWORK FOR THE FOLLOWING SECTIONS

David Tee for Circus Skills

Dean Beattie and Monica Golding for Lets Get Physical

Julia Holmes for Munch Bunch

Maggie Walker for Media Madness

The Comfy Cushion activity was inspired by an article in *Schools Out* which in turn was inspired by a visit to the BBC Blue Peter studio.

Thanks to the staff and children at the following clubs for their help with case studies

The Roft After School Club

Deeside Holiday Club

Woodchurch High School After School Club

COOL CREATIONS

# Fabric Painting

## Why we like it

Fabric painting enables you to be as creative and funky as you like with your designs and even if you are not a great artist you can create something unique. You may want to link into a theme such as Valentines Day, zodiac signs, a sporting event, an environmental campaign or you may prefer an abstract design like a Jackson Pollock painting (and if you don't know who he is, find out! You may even like his designs and decide to do something similar). Some of the most effective designs employ a minimalist approach and if you don't fancy drawing your own design you can use a template or stencils. But at the end of the session you will have created something unique to take home or to wear at the fashion show.

## What you might need

Plain cotton T-shirt, vest top, shorts, head band etc

Fabric paint

Fabric pens

Paint brush

Iron

Ironing board

Piece of cardboard

Drawing pins

Overall or old shirt to protect you

Old newspapers to protect the surface you are working on.

## How many can do it

1–14 depending on the table space available.

## Where you can do it

It is best done indoors in case of sudden gusts of wind blowing dust or the sun drying the paint too quickly.

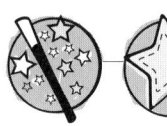

## How you can do it

**1.** Ensure the cloth is both clean and dry. If you are using a new T-shirt it must be washed first to remove the dressing, but be sure to iron it flat before starting to paint on it.

**2.** Try your design on paper first, it is easier to make changes at this stage if necessary.

**3.** When you are satisfied with the design, pin the item you are going to paint onto a cardboard sheet so that you have a taut surface to work on. The cardboard also prevents the paint going through the fabric onto the other side.

**4.** If necessary draw your design onto the fabric using an ordinary pencil or dressmakers chalk. Or if you feel confident enough, use a fabric pen.

**5.** Start by painting the light colours first and then move on to the darker ones once the light ones have dried, otherwise you will get smudges.

**6.** Let your design dry according to the manufacturer's instructions. Directions may vary with different makes so please read them carefully.

**7.** To set the fabric paint, place a clean dry cloth over the design and then iron it with the temperature set for cotton. Again follow the manufacturer's instructions carefully for best results.

### Safety Check
Be very careful when using the iron, and remember to let it cool before putting it away. Always read the manufacturers instructions on the paints carefully and follow them to ensure success.

COOL CREATIONS

## Useful Tips

**1.** Remember you can mix fabric paints just as you do ordinary paints to get different colours. Try to use an old T shirt or vest top to start with and experiment with simple designs or just writing slogans. Once you have mastered the technique be bold and do your own thing .

**2.** NES Arnold has a good selection of paints via mail order, or the following are available in most good art and craft shops and some toy shops:

Tulip Pearl 3D Paints are in psychedelic colours

Dylon Fabric Paint Pens are good for outlining or writing.

Dylon Fabric Paint is a good all round fabric paint

Deco Art Craft Twinkles is, as the name suggests, a glittery paint.

## Spotlight

It was agreed at one of the monthly meetings of 'Club 10 to 14' that they needed an identity, so they came up with a logo see page 2. It was then decided that each member of the club would paint the logo onto a piece of clothing of their choice. Craft aprons, T-shirts or sweat shirts, baseball caps and hair bands were just some of the items painted. Those who were good at drawing made templates for others who had limited drawing skills, but everyone was able to sport the club logo on some piece of clothing.

## What next?

As well as using fabric paints on fashion items, they can be used on soft furnishings to make individual cushions or decorate edges of curtains, pillow cases etc.

Why not link in to the cat walk section in this book and include your cool creations in the fashion show?

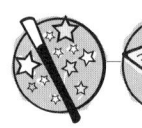

CAN DO

# Friendship Bracelet & Hair Braiding

## Why we like it

Plaiting threads to make friendship bracelets, chokers and hair bands as well as braiding hair is both fun and fashionable. You don't have to practice for long before you become an expert at the craft and then, once you have mastered the art you can experiment with different techniques.

## What you might need

Embroidery thread in different colours
Safety pin
Cushion, small enough to rest on your lap but heavy enough to stay firm when the threads are taut.
Scissors
Comb
Some glass beads (optional).

## How many can do it

Making a bracelet is done individually but hair braiding needs two people.

## Where can you do it

The beauty of these activities is they can be done anywhere.

### Useful Tips

Once you are proficient you can dispense with the cushion and possibly even pin the threads to your jeans, but don't try this on any thin fragile material because it will tear!

You can experiment with alternative fastenings such as making a loop at one end to fasten over a bead at the other. Once you can plait you can also braid hair.

— COOL CREATIONS —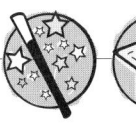

## How you can do it

### Bracelet

**1.** Measure loosely around the wrist, double the length and add 14 cm.

**2.** Cut 2 pieces of each of the three different colours to this length which will be roughly 374 cm The more threads you use the thicker the bracelet will be.

**3.** Knot all the threads together leaving a 10 cm tassel above the knot.

**4.** Pin through the knot with the safety pin and then pin onto the cushion.

**5.** Place the cushion on your knee.

**6.** Spread the three different coloured threads out see Fig.1

**7.** Take colour A over colour B, then colour C over colour A, then B over C and A over B colour.

See Figs. 2 and 3 This is much easier to see when you are using coloured threads. You are now plaiting!

**8.** Continue in this manner until you have the required length for your bracelet.

**9.** Tie a knot at the end of the plait.

**10.** Cut the bottom threads to the same length as the tassel at the top.

**11.** Thread a glass or wooden bead onto each coloured thread and then tie a knot large enough to prevent the beads slipping off.

**12.** Trim the knot end using sharp scissors.

**13.** You now have a friendship bracelet that you can secure using a simple knot.

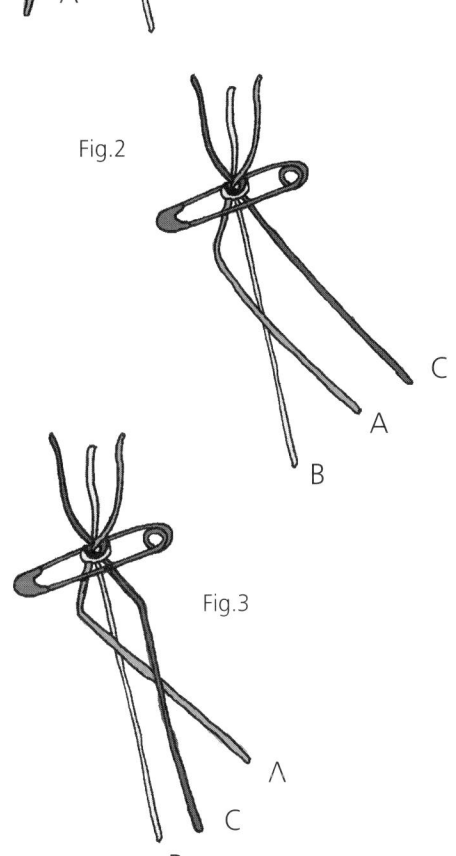

### Safety Check

You will need to use sharp scissors to cut the threads when you have tied the knots so be extra careful with these.

If hair braids are left on for more than a few days you should use a moisturising spray to keep the scalp supple.

 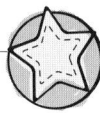

CAN DO

### Hair Braiding

This needs two people—one to do the braiding the other to have their hair braided. It is extremely difficult to plait your own hair. Use the same method as you did for the friendship bracelet but use strands of hair instead of the thread. Remember the thicker the strand the thicker the braid will be. When you come to the end of the braid secure it with a coloured band and then bind it with coloured thread or ribbon.

### Spotlight—Did You Know?

In the days of Marie Antoinette hair styles were very extravagant, often reaching two feet in height with the aid of padding. Considerable time was needed to erect these elaborate hair styles which sometimes contained extraordinary adornments such as models of battles, coaches and horses and windmills, so women slept with their necks on wooden blocks to protect the creation. Styles were only redone every two or three months so you can just imagine the amount of livestock which had taken up residence in the hair by then. It is said that one lady even had a mouse living in her hair!

### What next?

These activities can be used as a springboard for investigating hairstyles and fashions of different cultures from around the world and hair braiding provides a lead-in to sessions on hair care and hygiene in general.

COOL CREATIONS

# Making Faces

## Why we like it

Face painting is fun and what better reason is there for doing any activity? Make-up can transform a human face into something horrible or quite beautiful, in a very short space of time. Face painting allows you to take a flight of fancy and let go of your inhibitions and be who or what you want, for a while anyway. It can also be used as the basis for a wide range of other artistic and dramatic activities.

## How many can do it

2+. Although you can do your own makeup it is more fun to work in pairs, this way you need less mirrors too.

## Where can you do it

This activity can take place both indoors and outside.

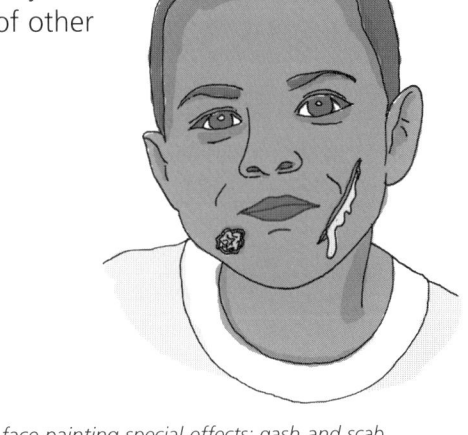

*face painting special effects: gash and scab*

## What you might need

Face paint crayons, however it is difficult to create strong colours with these and they can be quite difficult to remove.
Or
Left over street makeup which is ordinary foundation, eyeshadow, lipstick etc. available from mothers, aunts, sisters etc. or from the discontinued lines in the make-up department of your local chemist shop. This has the advantage of being either free or relatively inexpensive but the colours will be limited. You may also find that boys refuse to use them as they are seen as girls things!
Or
Face paints in as many different colours as you can afford. The most popular makes are Snazaroo, Grimas and Aquacolour (see web site details). These are all non toxic and made specially for face painting and stage make-up.

You can of course use a combination of all three if you want to.

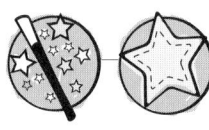

## What you might need cntd.

Mirror

Black eye pencil

Red lip pencil

Pencil sharpener

Make-up brushes. A fine one for eye lining and a slightly thicker one for lips and eyelids. You will need a 6 mm brush for highlights and blending and a 12mm brush for larger areas.

Make-up sponges

Cocktail sticks

Cotton buds

Tissues

Cotton wool

Moisturising cream or baby lotion

Soap

Water

Towel

Hair band

Soft lead pencil and drawing paper

For special effects you will need:

Wax

Fake blood

Bran flakes

Water soluble glue.

## How you can do it

1. If you are going to wear makeup for a prolonged length of time it is best to use a light moisturising cream on the face first as this will help to protect the skin and make it easier to remove the make up at a later stage.

2. Draw hair back from the face and secure with a head band.

3. Put a protective cover round the neck and shoulders, either a towel or tissues.

4. Decide which face you want to create. Will it be an animal or a clown, or a witch or a wizard?

5. There are several good books with face paint designs and brand name face paints also come with instruction sheets and ideas for designs (see website details).

6. Draw a template of your chosen design on a piece of paper. Fill in the lines and colours you will be using with felt pens and/or paint. It is much easier to alter a line or change a colour on a drawing than it is on a face.

7. You could also try the following home-made special effects:

### A Gash

Take a small piece of wax and mould it into an oblong. (Kryoplan Special Wax or Naturo Plasto are both self adhesive).

Press it firmly onto clean, dry skin.

Blend the edges of the wax using either a cocktail stick or your finger.

With a cocktail stick pick out some of the wax from the middle to form a channel.

With a paint brush line the gash with dark red paint.

Add a little fake blood to finish off the effect.

### A Scab

Stick a crushed bran flake onto clean dry skin using a small amount of water soluble glue.

Add a touch of red paint to create the impression of an oozing sore and colour round the edges with very small amounts of red, grey and green paint to blend it into the skin.

COOL CREATIONS

## Spotlight—Did You Know?

Since the time of the ancient Egyptians cosmetics have been worn by both men and women. In ancient tribes body and face painting had cultural meanings attached to it often depicting social status within the community. Certain colours were significant. Yellow meant a man had lived his life and would fight to the finish and green under the eyes was to make him see better in the dark!

Did you know that in the 18th century the British parliament passed a law condemning the use of lipstick and any woman found guilty of seducing a man into matrimony by cosmetic means could be tried for witchcraft. However by World War II opinion had gone full circle and it became a patriotic duty for women to 'put their face on' to boost the morale of the soldiers.

## Useful Tips

If you have used water soluble paint remove it with soap and water. For street-make up and grease paint use cotton wool and baby lotion to remove. The wax and bran flakes can be removed by gently easing off the skin followed by a wash with soap and water or cleansing with baby lotion as appropriate.

Remember when you are buying paints that you are likely to use more black and white paint than any other colours, so buy extra.

## What next?

Why not experiment with clown make up and link into the circus skills section and when you have developed your expertise use your skills to make money by doing face painting at local events.
Special wax and face paints can be bought from theatre shops or by mail order via the internet. Check out the following addresses:
*www.covent-garden.co.uk/SITES/charlesfox/packages/facepainter.html*
*www.creationmodels.co.uk/makeup/*
*www.snazaroo.com/ideas.htm*

Further reading:
*The Usborne Book of Dressing Up, Costumes, Masks and Face Painting,* by Cheryl Evans and Paula Borton, published by Usborne, 1993, ISBN 0-74601-504-6.

*Face Painting,* by Jaqueline Russon, published by Henderson, 1996. ISBN 1-85597-621-8.

*Face Painting,* by Lynsy Pinsent, published by Apple, 1993. ISBN 1-85076-461-1.

## Safety Check

Always test the make up on the inside of your wrist before using it on your face. If you have not had an allergic reaction after an hour it is safe to continue. It would be sensible to do the allergy test a few days before you plan a make up session. Take great care when using any brushes or pencils near the eyes. Let the one being made up do that bit for themselves.

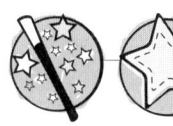

CAN DO

# Putting on the Style

## Why we like it

Organising a fashion show is easy, you don't have to learn lines or remember complicated stage directions, it can cover a variety of themes and it doesn't cost anything. It involves a lot of people in different capacities and with different skills so that those who enjoy performing can do so and those who don't can take an equally important and skilful backstage roll. A successful show relies on team work and co-operation.

## How many can do it

A fashion show can be put on with as few as 10 but it is better if you have a larger number as this gives the models more time to change their costumes.

## Where you can do it

It can be done both indoors and outside depending on the weather.

## How you can do it

**1.** Select your theme. Will it be fashion from outer space, the history of fashion from cave man to present day, sports gear or a trip down memory lane for parents in the audience with the fashion of yesteryear? I am sure you will come up with innovative ideas of your own.

**2.** Decide who the models are going to be. The beauty of organising your own fashion show is that models can be any shape or size, it really doesn't matter.

**3.** Make the costumes, unless they are already made in which case they may need some adjusting to fit the models.

**4.** Select dressers to help models in and out of their costumes and to make sure accessories and props are to hand.

**5.** Choose a make up artist, you may need several if the theme requires exotic make up.

**6.** Ask a hairdresser to help with hair styling, wigs, hair pieces etc.

**7.** Look for someone to take charge of the music. Select music appropriate to the theme if possible.

**8.** Find a compere to welcome the audience and to introduce the models.

**9.** Write the script for the compere which should name the model and describe the outfit they are wearing for example, 'The 'in' colour on Venus this autumn is hot orange and here we have Jo in a dazzling off-the-shoulder creation suitable for holidays by the sea of Lunaria ...'

**10.** Design the catwalk. Ideally this should be a T shape, approximately 13 metres long with the bar at the end approximately 4 metres long, but again this depends on the space you have. The cat walk can be marked out using chalk, a length of rope or, for a dramatic effect, you can use fairy lights.

**11.** Choreograph the moves: the models can dance, turn cartwheels or do summersaults down the cat walk or they can just walk, it depends on the theme.

**12.** Set the screens up to change behind if the show is outdoors or to hide the door to the changing room if performing indoors.

## Useful Tips

Most charity shops will sell you a bag of clothes for £1 if you tell them what it is for and if you ask for as many of their glamorous outfits as they can spare they usually oblige. Jumble sales and requests to parents can also be fruitful. Old jackets, hats, scarves and shoes are particularly useful items to have in a dressing up box as are foil, black bin bags and bubble wrap.

Glue, staples, iron on wonder web and sticky tape can be used instead of sewing if you are in a hurry or don't actually like sewing!

CAN DO

## Snapshot

The Roft after school club put on a fashion show to celebrate 50 years since the end of the Second World war. Young people were asked to talk to the older generation in their community who had lived through the war to see what their experiences were. Some of the elderly people had kept costumes, hats and shoes as well as uniforms that they loaned out for the day. The music included songs such as 'It's a Long Way to Tipperary' and 'Lily Marlene'. At the end of the show, afternoon tea was served by waitresses and waiters dressed in period costume. Fortunately for the guests tea was not based on war time rations! Following the show the audience were invited to join in with an old fashioned sing song.

The show helped to build self-confidence and self- esteem especially in those who were naturally less outgoing. There were many backstage roles for those not wanting to be right in the spotlight: production manager, make up artist, dresser, script writer etc. After the fashion show the group went on to organise an old time music hall show with several young people taking very active parts after building up their confidence in the fashion show.

## Safety Check

There is nothing particularly hazardous in this activity but make sure clothes are clean and that the cable from the CD player is well away from the models. If the cat walk is raised take care with acrobatic movements. If using fairy lights to mark out the catwalk ensure the wiring is in good condition and that no one is likely to trip over them. Fairy lights can add a delightful touch of fantasy to a show so it is worthwhile taking the extra care.

## What next?

A fashion show is a good introduction to drama activities.
The following books are useful guides to improvisation and scripted drama.
*Dramattack!* by Donald C. Stewart, published by Russell House Publishing, 1999.
ISBN 1-89892-422-8
*Drama with Children* by Sarah Phillips, published by Oxford University Press, 1999.
ISBN 0-19437-220-0

COOL CREATIONS

## Fun with Photos

### Why we like it

People love to take photographs, of themselves or their friends, of a group or an activity or a series of events that happen. Taking photographs on trips out is also fun and provides a picture story of what they may have done. This will stimulate your creativity and imagination and encourage group activity.

### How many can do it

1–5 people in small groups.

One person or a small group working together to take it in turns to use the camera or be part of the production team.

### Where you can do it

Indoors or outdoors, depending on what you want to take pictures of—people or places or 'things'. Remember you need a well-lit place indoors, preferably with a flash camera, and a sunny day is best for outdoors.

### What you may need

Polaroid or disposable camera

Display boards, card and large coloured paper

Mounts

Photo Albums

Camera films and access to film developing

Pritt stick

Useful tip

Use a camera you are happy to use. An automatic camera with flash is ideal. You can borrow one or buy one. Disposable cameras are great and can often be bought in bulk. Try writing to local stores and companies that sell them, ask for donations of unused stock, promotional items or end-of-line products.

Familiarise yourselves with how to use the camera you have chosen

Use 100 ASA for bright weather and 400 ASA for moving images e.g. sports activity

Decide how you will get the films developed: one hour printing for more instant fun or over night. The cheaper option allows you to plan your presentation. You can send films away by post and you will receive free films in return and pay less overall.

CAN DO

## How you can do it

An ideal way to start planning what to do is to sit down informally as a group and decide a plan of action. For example:

What photographs do you want to take and where?
What story do you want to tell?
How do you want to represent that story, for example, collage, framed photographs, posters or albums?

You may all have different ideas that are good—use your thoughts and ideas to create one or more activities.

Investigate access to a local photographic studio. A local community resource may exist to help with developing. They may let you all use the facilities so you can plan a day or afternoon out of the club to do this. A parent may be able to help—ask around.
Here are some ideas:

Portraits of club members

Photo-montage of the club—The people and the place

Photographs of an activity that day, for example, a football match, cooking session or a trip out

A still-life study, for example, something in the club that is of interest to the photographer(s)

Decide who will take, and how to take, the photographs and start shooting, Check the lighting, check the subjects are happy to have their picture taken (remember some people don't like to have their photograph taken) and after the film is finished, consider if you need to take some more. When all the films are taken, keep them safe, and decide who and how, they will be developed. And don't forget to collect them or remember when they are due back in the post.

In the meantime, the group can start to plan their presentation, whatever it may be. When the photos are collected, select and sort them according to quality. Some photos are at their best when they are out of focus or blurred. Others are better because of the colours they show. Remember that you often only get one or two good photos per film.

Choosing what to do with the photos also depends on how they come out - more ideas may spring from this too.

### Safety Check

Photography is a safe activity unless you are planning to develop your own films. Supervision is needed throughout all sessions in the dark room and you will need technical assistance and support, which many local community resources will offer. Enquire how many can be together at any one time and plan ratios accordingly.

COOL CREATIONS

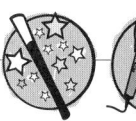

## Spotlight

Photographs are a good way of documenting what goes on in your setting and telling stories. You can use photos as a historical record, for publicity, for individuals to make a record of their lives, a personal profile, to develop their sense of family or for special occasions. Encourage everyone to bring their favourite photos in from home of friends and family and this will help spark off new ideas and themes to work with.

Fig.1

Fig.2

## Snapshot

A group of 10–14 year olds decided to compile a colour photo-montage of their club and activities they had undertaken. This included everything from football to cooking and trips out to festival days. They took a number of films and developed them at the local chemist. They chose ten of the best and these were enlarged to a size of 25 x 20 cm and mounted on card with edging (see fig.1).
Placing them on the largest wall they used each photograph as an activity theme, for example, the best football picture became the focus for all the other football photos. The photos were stuck on larger pieces of coloured paper, which created a backdrop to the whole display. By each photo the young people wrote their thoughts and gave each display a title: 'Football Crazy' and 'Cool Cooks', for example. This represented a whole term of activities and enabled all the young people to have their pictures on display (see fig.2).

## What next?

Collage works well to tell a story or bring a photograph or series of photographs to life. Other things can be done to photos too, such as blowing them up, in part or total, on a photocopier. Experiment with black and white and colour film.

CAN DO

# Newspaper Know-How

## Why we like it

Producing your own newspaper is great fun and can involve everyone. It provides an opportunity to talk about yourselves and to find out what is going on around you in the community.

Newspapers provide information exchange and can stimulate discussion. In a world ever more technical, a newspaper is a tangible record for you to keep.

## How many can do it

You will need an editorial group—up to 3–4 young people and volunteers for features and stories. Everyone can play a part. Some may do photographs or illustrations or create ideas for themes for each edition. Some may be happy to interview and write up stories.

## Where you can do it

Indoors is best, where there is lots of space, for example, on a tabletop or on the floor if it is safe and clean.

## What you might need

Paper
Pencils and pens
Eraser
Polaroid camera
Scissors
Glue
Access to personal computer, if possible.

COOL CREATIONS

## How you can do it

Get everyone to decide what they want to call their newspaper and what sort of paper it will be. For example, 'Playclub Times' or 'Kids' Clubs Review' would be catchy. Do you want the content to be serious and informative, chatty or informal or a mixture of both?

Agree on a chief editor to lead the editorial group. He or she will encourage and gather ideas and opinions from all the others. Once this is done, call an editorial group meeting to finalise plans.

The agreed content could include:

News Stories

Profiles

Interviews

Features, for examples, Fashion and Music

Cartoons

Drawings

Sport

Jokes

Adverts

Horoscopes

Photographs

Decide who will do what. Check out everyone's particular interest and skills—you may have a brilliant artist on site that would be happy to compile cartoons. Plan a few stories and interviews and decide who will do them and write them up. You may decide to do a weekly or monthly newsletter, with ongoing or separate themes.

Once you have gathered enough material to fill 4–8 sides of A4 paper (or A3 if you are ambitious!) have another editorial team meeting. Decide on final content and format. You may wish to hand-write, type or word process the features and literally stick them down on the paper, that is, cut and paste.

If your setting has access to a personal computer you can use one of the various desktop publishing packages to aid production. Once all the pages are in place, photocopy or print as many copies as you need to distribute amongst yourselves, to parents, other agencies and contacts in the area. Think who your newspaper is aimed at and make sure all those interested get a copy!

CAN DO

## Snapshot

'COOL KIDS NEWS' is produced monthly by a group of 12–14 year olds. The editorial team of two boys and two girls decided on the themes for the year. Within the 8 page newspaper they chose to do 'News & views, 'Fashion and Music ' features, a profile page', 'What It's Like To Be Me, a cartoon strip, a role-model interview and a joke slot. Photographs are taken and used for the fashion page and to identify the individuals on the profile page and role model interview. The layout looks like the one on page 16.

The team allocated each section to an individual with the appropriate skills. They chose to do as many of the twelve monthly newsletters that they could commit to, giving each person enough time to compile and complete the task. The team allowed a week of after-school sessions to complete the final draft.

## What next?

You might want to swap stories with other groups in your area or feature joint activities. Meanwhile other young people can be writing horoscopes, writing sports reports and taking photographs.

## Useful Tips

Think of a catchy title

Be really creative

Make sure that material is appropriate for the age range and potential readers

Check how and where interviews are taking place—make sure they are in a safe environment and are supervised if appropriate

Get feedback from the readers by starting a feedback column and ensure your readers are enjoying the newspaper

Establish ground rules about not publishing anything that would cause offence

## Spotlight—Using Information Exchange

Producing a newspaper can lead to bigger things: Attracting people into the club, sponsorship of activities or helping young people with topical and tricky issues that they have to confront in their lives. Providing information is key to enabling and ensuring support for young people and the research element can be as important as the finished product. The young editors and journalists should hold ownership of the editorial process. Adult support might be required for technical aspects.

COOL CREATIONS

## Roving Reporters

### Why we like it

By interviewing others you find out about other people's views and what is going on in the wider community. You can use this activity to make new contacts, to promote what is happening in your setting, or to get ideas for other things to do.

### How many can do it

An individual can do it alone or for safety's sake, 'rove' in pairs or groups, especially if away from supervision. If you don't have access to more than one tape recorder, take it in turns to share equipment.

### What you might need

Cassette tapes

Tape recorder with microphone or ('walkman' with microphone)

Pens and paper.

### Where you can do it

The reporters may want to 'rove' around your own setting and interview different people or you may choose to go out into the community. Key considerations are time of day and weather conditions—it is probably best when it is light and not raining! When outdoors, it maybe better to have arranged a rendezvous because you will need as little background noise as possible. Noise from traffic or people will distract you from the task in hand and ruin any tape you produce. A local park or community centre may be a good location but ask permission to use premises.

CAN DO

## How you can do it

The 'roving reporters' may decide on a group or individual themes. These could include, for example:

'Who's who in our club'

    A getting to know you session

What's going on in our community?'

    Getting to know key people in the community, for example, police, a local footballer or a community representative.

    Getting to know our local hot-spots by interviewing staff from local facilities, for example, an internet-cafe, a coffee-bar or a leisure complex

For each theme the one or two persons involved need to draw up a schedule of questions for interviewing.

A schedule of Questions might include:

Please identify yourself by giving us: your name and who you work for, job title and your role responsibilities.

'What do you offer for young people in this area?'

'How much do you charge and do you have to be a member?'

'What other activities are planned for the future?'

'Where do we get further information?'

Think about what questions you want to ask and to whom. Make sure that they are polite and appropriate to the individual in question.

Once all the activities are recorded you may choose to transcribe the interviews onto paper or put them into a newsletter or club newspaper. This will enable you to share information with everyone in the club—novel way of learning about each other and the local area! Think of innovative ways of presenting the material—whether transcribed on paper or played back to other members of the club.

### Safety Check

Be aware of who and how you interview—make sure everyone is safe.

### Useful Tips

Be organised. Have the questions ready

Practice asking questions on each other

For each session, use a new tape and label it well with the subject, interviewee, date and time of interview

Practice asking questions that don't allow for yes or no answers. For example, instead of asking 'Do you like living here?' ask, 'What's the best and worst things about living here?'

COOL CREATIONS

## Snapshot

Three 14 year olds from Smart kids club decided they wanted to write an article on a new organic food bar that had recently opened in town called 'Smooth Food'. Firstly they contacted the manager and explained who they were and what they wanted to do and explained it would be good publicity for 'Smooth Food'. The Manager was very enthusiastic and offered a free meal after the interview.

The trio then started to plan what questions they were to ask. To prepare for the interview they did research into what organic food was, into any local competition and the need for the shop in their area.

The interview took about half an hour, and on finishing, they thanked the manager for his participation and explained that the recorded interview would be typed for his approval.

When seeing the finished article the manager agreed for his interview to be published and was very grateful for the positive coverage it produced for 'Smooth Food'.

## Spotlight—Promoting Positive Behaviour

Most people are naturally inquisitive and this activity builds on natural motivation to find out about others, giving a format and a context for asking questions. By interviewing other people in the community you can find out about what life is like for others who live and work nearby. This can lead to greater tolerance, understanding and increased support for others, and an increased sense of self, citizenship and community for the reporters.

## What next?

Keep up with local and national news for any interesting stories to cover.

Why not think of a theme for your newsletter, for example, Christmas, or What to do in summer, for example.

CAN DO

## Video Ventures

### Why we like it

Video can be used as a one-off activity or to document the life of a particular group or setting. As a medium, video can be fun and glamorous but needs some technical expertise and occasional supervision by adults. It can make for a great group activity or can be done in pairs.

Making a video film can be very rewarding and can create interest and excitement and boost the self-image of those involved. As a co-operative activity, it encourages teamwork and clear communication.

It can also be a very powerful tool when used to explore and investigate issues of concern and interest to young people and their communities.

### How many can do it

Depending on the type of video you are producing, allocate the appropriate number of people to the activity, for example, a simple news story could be led by two people, a documentary or fictional story would need more people.

### Where you can do it

Both indoors and outdoors depending on the weather and what type of video you are planning. Use of lights indoors will help if there is a poor source of natural light. Be somewhere quiet! It is also important to check for sound (make sure it is working!).

### What you might need

VHS tape cartridge
Camcorder (with power pack and rechargeable batteries)
VHS tape cartridge adapter
Domestic VHS recorder
Television
Video lights
Pen and paper.

COOL CREATIONS

## How you can do it

Let everyone who wants to use the camcorder have a go, giving each of them an opportunity to influence what is produced. It is good to devise some kind of script or story before you start so everyone involved knows what is planned. Creating a crew for each type of video film is ideal. A typical crew might include:

A writer of the story or script
The video filmmaker who films
A director (who directs)
An assistant to the director (who helps)
A general assistant (who runs around on errands, such as getting props)

The story line for each type of activity might include:

An introduction: what the video is about
A main body of content
An ending: saying what was said

The writer is responsible, with the help of others, for developing the story line. The length of video footage will vary. Start small initially and see how you get on. As time goes by, be more ambitious and lengthen your video. You can either play back on camera or via a TV, as you go along, re-tape over sections that you are not happy with.

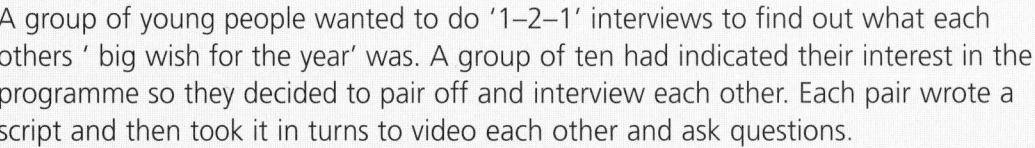

CAN DO

## Snapshot

### '1–2–1'

A group of young people wanted to do '1–2–1' interviews to find out what each others ' big wish for the year' was. A group of ten had indicated their interest in the programme so they decided to pair off and interview each other. Each pair wrote a script and then took it in turns to video each other and ask questions.

'What is your big wish for your year? ' was the question. 'I want to go to Jamaica' came one reply. 'I want to pass my exams' was another and 'I'd love to learn to fly' yet another.

By the end of the twenty interviews, the team had compiled a relatively short video of their aspirations which was good fun to watch and helped them to start thinking about what they were doing that year. Would they achieve their ambitions or were they pure fantasy? Either way, they had an enjoyable time finding out about each other and learning about their different aspirations.

## What next?

Try several different types of video for example:

Running a news story

Doing a documentary film

Creating a story or drama

Filming an activity indoors

Following an outdoor event, such as, a football match

Doing an interview

Filming role-play

You may decide to do one or all of the different types of video. In time, you will be compiling a comprehensive video diary and library of, and for, the club. Remember to look back after 6–9 months and see how things may or may not have changed! Either way, you will have more fun recalling events.

## Useful Tips

Speak to local libraries, community centres or parents to see if they will lend you equipment in order to keep down costs.

Don't forget continuity, especially if you are videoing a drama. You want everything to stay the same from shot to shot! The assistant to the director can help on this one.

Avoid filming bright lights as it will affect the video.

Do a few practice runs with one tape as you can always film over your first or second attempts.

COOL CREATIONS

# Wicked Walls

## Why we like it

In many discos and clubs these days images are projected onto the walls using film projectors and transparencies. The same effect can be achieved by using this simpler and cheaper method. The images can cover any topic from sport and pop to food and fashion, and they can be changed regularly. It leaves scope for the development of ideas by creative minds, such as drawing round the images and painting the scene to from a mural. Alternatively images can be projected onto a white marker board and pictures created using marker board pens. This has the advantage of being easily removed and mistakes can be rectified quickly. The pictures can be based on themes or can be a complete hotch potch of freely chosen images.

## How many can do it

One or more, but preferably no more than 6 working on an image at any one time.

## Where you can do it

Indoors—although one person I know projected silhouette images onto a whitewashed garden wall at night to mark the outlines, and then painted them in daylight.

## What you might need

Access to a photocopier that will also do transparencies (sometimes called acetates) for an overhead projector.

An overhead projector

Magazines, books and photographs

Pencils

Coloured paints

White marker board

White board pens in a variety of colours.

CAN DO

## How you can do it

Select your image. Depending on the size of the picture you may need to enlarge it on a photocopier before making the transparency

As all photocopiers are different you will need to make the transparency by following the instructions in the photocopier's instruction manual or go to a print shop where they will do it for you (for a fee of course!).

Place the transparency on the overhead projector and experiment with the focus and the distance from the wall or white marker board. The further away the larger the image will be.

You can stop here if you want, but if you want to produce a semi permanent mural you will need to:

Draw round the image projected onto the wall using a soft pencil or marker pen

Fill-in using acrylic paints.

### Useful Tips

If you are going on to produce a mural try to find a picture that has clear outlines and shapes, as they will be much easier to follow. If your picture does not cover the whole wall you may like to paint a border round it to give a more professional finish. Make sure the marker pens are those specifically for use on white marker board, otherwise you will damage the board permanently as they will not wipe off.

Murals on a wall can be easily removed with a big paintbrush or roller and a tin of emulsion paint, and then you can start all over again.

### Snapshot

'Our community' was the title of a holiday club's mural. They divided the wall measurement into four equal parts and then bought four pieces of hardboard cut to measure. The hardboard was light enough to handle and easily painted with matt white emulsion. (The year before they used MDF which was much too heavy to handle and required a joiner to fix it to the wall.) The overall design was divided and those who wanted to be involved in the project selected which bits to work on. Some images were taken using the above techniques, others were drawn freehand. It was an ongoing project though the holiday. Participation was voluntary and there were not set times for 'Mural Making'—It was done as and when the mood took them. It was completed over six weeks of the summer holiday and now resides in the local library.

COOL CREATIONS

## Safety Check

You will need to ensure the electricity cable from the overhead projector is safety secured so that no one can trip over it.

If you are painting please remember protective clothing for yourself and newspaper to protect the floor and surrounding areas.

## What next?

This activity fits in well with the Fun with Photos section of this book. Marker board murals or those about to be erased can be captured for posterity on camera or conversely images taken in the Fun with Photos sessions can be used to create wicked walls images.

CAN DO

# New for Old

## Why we like it

By mastering the art of decoupage you can dramatically transform the appearance of lots of items such as trays, old biscuit tins, waste paper bins, etc. It is an inexpensive way to modernise and jazz up things which look as though they are past their sell by date! This technique can be used on almost any surface: wood, metal, plastic, paper, pottery and even melamine (such as old table mats) You can use your imagination to the full by selecting different background colours and cut out designs from gift wrapping paper, magazines, wallpaper, cards, tickets, labels or stamps, you can even add a bit of glitter and some sequins if you want to. It is an inexpensive art form which gives scope for the imagination and allows those who are not very good at drawing to produce decorated items which look great.

## What you might need

Tray, storage tin, box, waste bin or whatever takes your fancy.

Small sharp scissors

Pictures from gift wrapping paper, magazines, catalogues, birthday cards, etc. These can be coloured or black and white depending on the effect you want to create.

Paint brushes: two medium sized ones for the emulsion paint and varnish and one small one for the glue

Fine sand paper

Glue, water based PVA

Matt emulsion paint

Wallpaper seam roller (optional)

Kitchen paper towel or sponge

Clear matt or silk finish water based varnish.

## How many can do it

1+

## Where can you do it

Preferably indoors to avoid dust blowing onto the paint or varnish.

COOL CREATIONS

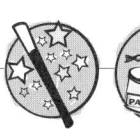

## How you can do it

**1.** Lightly sand down the surface to be treated with fine grade sand paper. This is not necessary if you are working on paper.

**2.** Then wash the surface to be covered to make sure all dust and grease have been removed from the surface.

**3.** When dry, use a medium sized paint brush to paint the surface with matt emulsion in your chosen colour.

**4.** Cut out your fun pictures carefully.

**5.** Decide on the pattern for the decoration—will some pictures or motifs overlap or will they be spaced out?

**6.** Using the small paint brush carefully spread the PVA glue over the back of the first picture and stick it in place.

**7.** Press down firmly with a wallpaper seam roller if you have one, otherwise use kitchen paper or a sponge to make sure there are no bubbles or wrinkles.

**8.** Continue in this way until you have achieved the required effect.

**9.** You must then leave the design to dry overnight.

**10.** Now you can varnish the item using a satin or matt finish varnish.

**11.** You will need at least three coats of varnish. It is important to let each coat dry thoroughly and to rub down lightly with very fine sand paper between coats. If you are using glitter add it to the coats of varnish.

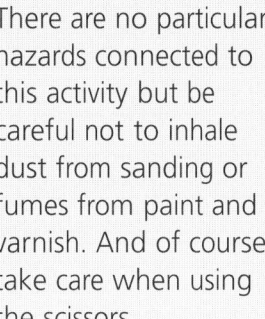

**Safety Check**

There are no particular hazards connected to this activity but be careful not to inhale dust from sanding or fumes from paint and varnish. And of course take care when using the scissors.

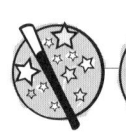

CAN DO

## Snapshot

Tops Children's Centre was just starting up and had a limited amount of money for furniture so they bought very inexpensive folding tables from Ikea that had MDF tops. To cheer them up they decorated them to reflect the different cultures represented within the centre. The group working on the Chinese table chose Chinese lacquer red for the base and then cut out photographs concerning all things Chinese from travel brochures, cookery books and magazines. A parent who had been brought up in China during the cultural revolution also did some authentic Chinese calligraphy to add to the decoration. This was done in black ink on white paper and had to be sealed with a diluted PVA solution to prevent the ink from running before it could be added to the table top.

## What next?

If you decide to use foreign bank notes, stamps or labels, which may be in shorter supply than other motifs, it is better to use these on smaller items.

Once you have mastered the technique you could try revamping other larger items such as table tops, like the case study, or old screens and cupboard doors.

## Useful Tips

Try the technique out on paper plates first, just to get the hang of it. If these are a success you can always hang them on the wall.

If you use water based paint, glue and varnish you do not have to use expensive white spirit to clean your brushes, they can be cleaned in warm soapy water and then dried thoroughly.

Supermarkets and DIY stores sell packs of cheap paint brushes and most parents have odd half full tins of paint standing on their garage shelves which they will gladly hand over for a good cause. Alternatively, look for trial size pots of paint or ends of lines on the bargain counter.

Specific interest magazines from pop and sport, to fashion and film, will be readily available and a few sheets of gift wrapping paper, if required, won't break the bank. If you fancy some glitter and sequins try NES Arnold who have a wonderful selection.

Because you need several coats of varnish this activity cannot be completed in one session.

COOL CREATIONS

# Dough Designs

## Why we like it

Dough is a satisfying and fun medium to work with. It's like playing with plasticine or play dough but the end product is permanent and can be kept to decorate your own room or given away as a present or even sold at a fundraising event, especially around Christmas time. It is relatively easy and inexpensive to use but allows plenty of scope for the imagination. It is best to begin with a small simple design and as your skills develop progress to more complex ones. It is an activity that can be done in a couple of after school sessions so you quickly see the results of your work.

## What you might need

Flour
Salt
Water
Measuring mug
Mixing bowl
Rolling pin
Spoon
Pastry cutters of different shapes
Pastry brush
Fish slice
Baking tray
Water colour paints
Water colour varnish
Paint brushes: a very fine one,
a fine one and a medium sized one.

## How many can do it

This activity is best done individually at first but as your skills progress 4–5 could work together on a group plaque depicting a scene or garland of your choice.

## Where you can do it

As the dough will dry out quite quickly it is better to do this activity indoors.

CAN DO

## How you can do it

This quantity will make about 4 small decorations.

1. Put two mugs of flour into the mixing bowl
2. Add a mug of salt and mix both well together
3. Make a well in the centre and gradually add warm water until the dough is pliable. (It is best, and more fun, to mix the dough with your hands.)
4. Turn the dough out onto a floured surface and knead until it becomes smooth. If the dough drops too quickly when you hold it up then it is too moist so you should add more flour and knead it again.
5. Place the dough in a plastic bag and leave it to rest for at least 30 minutes.
6. Roll out the dough and using a pastry cutter cut out the shapes of your choice.
7. Using a fish slice lift the shapes onto a lightly oiled baking tray.
8. Bake in a cool oven 100°C, Gas Mark 1 for about two hours. All ovens vary so you will need to keep checking that the shapes are not burning. If the oven is too hot and the dough begins to rise prick it with a pin to let the air escape and lower the temperature. Alternatively they can be left to dry in a warm dry place such as an airing cupboard or on top of a radiator but this will take a longer time than in the oven, about 12 hours.
9. Once the shapes are dry you can paint them using water colours, enamel paints, or poster paints.
10. Once the paint is thoroughly dry varnish your design, you will need at least two coats of varnish. Watercolour varnish is best as it does not alter the colour of the paint. Some varnishes, even clear polyurethane has a slight brownish tinge to it.

## Useful Tips

Make sure the room you are working in is not too warm as heat, either from your hands or from the room will tend to dry the dough and make it difficult to work with. Cover the dough with a damp cloth when you are not working with it.

You can add a small quantity of vegetable oil, approximately 2 teaspoons, to the dough mixture if you are working in a very warm environment and need the dough to be more pliable.

For coloured dough add a few drops of food colouring to the mixture by making a small well in the centre, fold the dough over and then knead until the colour is evenly spread. However it is easier and more effective to paint your designs rather than colour the dough.

Different textures and patterns can be created using a variety of everyday objects such as buttons, a comb, kitchen fork, etc. If you are making a model that needs hair try pressing the dough through a garlic press.

Hanging designs such as Christmas tree decorations or name plates need a hole at the top that is large enough to thread a ribbon or cord through. Use a skewer or knitting needle to make the hole before the design is dried.

COOL CREATIONS

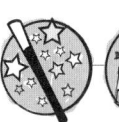

### Safety Check

Asthma sufferers should wear a mask when handling the dry flour. Sensitive skin may react adversely to the salt in the dough, if this happens use fine surgical gloves. If you are drying your designs in an oven you must use oven gloves to remove the trays after the drying out process.
You can use wall paper paste to make the dough more elastic, but you must make sure it does not contain fungicide as it is harmful.

### Snapshot

As a first birthday celebration for the Three Cs Club (Cool Caff Club) each member made a tile from salt dough approximately 8cm square. Tiles depicted their favourite activity so some used sporting images, others music, drama, etc. The maker's initials and date of birth were also included on each tile. When completed all the tiles were mounted onto a large frame that was then hung in the entrance for all to see. It required team work and co-operation and it meant that everyone was included in a work of art which would be there for years to come.

### What next?

Use different types of flour, including cornflour to create different textures.
There are some excellent books on Doughcraft which are available from your local library. Look in both the children's section and the adult craft sections.
Further reading:
*Christmas Doughcrafts* by Elizabeth Bang, published by Cassell, 1995. ISBN 0-30434-395-1
*Creative Doughcraft* by Patricia Hughes, published by Guild of Master Craftsmen, 1999. ISBN 1-86108-122-7
*Fairytale Doughcraft* by Anne Skødt, published by David Porteous, 1994. ISBN 1-87058-624-7

CAN DO

# Comfy Cushions

## Why we like it

Cushions, whether small or large, are satisfying and easy to make and can add a touch of comfort and luxury to any setting. Remnants of material or old pattern books, (material shops may be willing to give old ones to you), can easily be sewn into cushions. They can be made just for comfort as chair or floor cushions or for special occasions such as Mothers Day or Easter. They can be made with or without using a sewing machine but all require some sewing. Learning to use a needle and thread or a sewing machine are extremely useful life skills, for both sexes! The instructions that follow are for a cushion which does not require the use of a sewing machine.

### Cardigan Cushion

## What you might need

Old cardigan

Scraps of wool similar to the colour of the cardigan

A long ruler

Chalk

A bodkin (see useful tips) and a large eyed darning needle

Pins

Scissors

A stuffed inner pad slightly smaller than the cushion cover. This can be bought ready made or you can make your own.

## How many can do it

It can be done as a small group activity but is best done individually.

## Where you can do it

Preferably indoors but if it is a nice sunny day there is no reason why you can't do it outside as long as you have a table on which you can do the cutting and measuring.

## Safety Check

There are no particular hazards with this activity except of course the sharp end of the needle.

COOL CREATIONS

## How you can do it

**1.** Lay the cardigan out flat.

**2.** Do up the buttons and make sure the bottom edges of the cardigan are even.

**3.** Using the ruler, chalk a line across the cardigan from under one arm to the other.

**4.** Carefully cut along the line.

**5.** Turn the cardigan inside out.

**6.** Pin and stitch the cut edge using similar coloured wool and a large darning needle. Use small over stitch or backstitch to prevent it unravelling see Fig.1.

**7.** Stitch the bottom edge of the cardigan using the same coloured wool and the same stitch as the other edge, either over or backstitch, see Fig.1 and Fig.2.

**8.** Undo the buttons and turn the cardigan back to the right side so that the buttons are facing outwards.

**9.** Fill the cushion cover with a stuffed inner pad and do up the buttons.

To decorate with a tassel on each corner:

**1.** Cut a rectangular piece of card as wide as you want the tassels to be long.

**2.** Wind some wool round the card until it is as thick as you want the tassel to be leaving a long tail—at least 15 cm, see Fig.3.

**3.** Cut some wool about 20 cm in length and thread it onto a bodkin.

**4.** Pass the bodkin under the loops in the middle of the card a couple of times and tie firmly.

**5.** Remove the card, and holding the loops by the knot, cut through the opposite end.

**6.** To make the head of the tassel wind the end of the wool around the loops about 1 cm below the knot and fasten securely, see Fig.4.

**7.** Push the threaded needle through the knot at the top of the tassel and use the end to sew the tassel in place on the corners of the cushion. Repeat this process until you have 4 tassels—one for each corner.

**8.** Stitch the tassels on leaving a short length of wool so that they hang well.

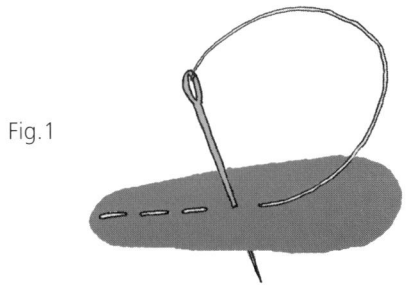

Fig.1

Fig.2

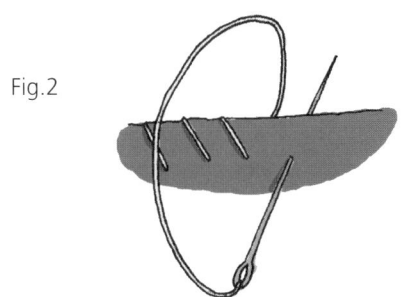

Fig.3

Fig.4

― CAN DO ―

## Useful Tips

A bodkin is easier to use than a needle for making the tassels. Bodkins are like needles but they have a rounded blunt end rather than a sharp point like a needle. Most needlework or haberdashery departments of larger stores will stock them.

As the buttons are a feature of this cushion design you may wish to change the original buttons on the cardigan for something more eye catching.

Remember the cushion does not have to be square and three quarter length cardigans make great oblong cushions. Try to use a cardigan which does not have a ribbed welt at the bottom.

A cardigan made from T-shirt type material is very effective if decorated with cut out designs in another colour or material which can then be sewn or glued on to the cushion cover. This technique is called applique.

## Snapshot

Cushions make useful presents or items to sell at fund raising events. Woodchurch High School on the Wirral has an after school club for 10–14 year olds and one of the most popular activities at the club last year was making cushions for mothers day presents. Lots of different materials were used, some were made from felt others from silk and decorated appropriately. Some small cushions were filled with dried lavender and rosemary that had been collected during the summer.

## What next?

The cardigan cushion is only one cushion idea, use your creativity and design and make a whole range for different purposes. Floor cushions add a homely and comfortable feel to an area meant for relaxation. Experiment with different fillings such as polystyrene balls, foam bits or even cut up old tights (though it can be a bit tedious doing this for a large floor cushion).

COOL CREATIONS

# Kick Rounders

## Why we like it

This is a fun and enjoyable way of using your football skills in a different way to the way you would use them in a game of football. This game combines speed and agility, while helping to develop co-ordination.

It is inclusive in design and requires very little equipment or understanding of rules, it encourages players to work together as a team, co-operating to ensure you field well enough to get the other team out quickly and ensure that your team scores the most runs.

The simple skills used during the game can be extended to most team sports. It is an enjoyable way of being active.

## What you might need

1 football or similar sized ball that can be kicked
6 cones, markers or chalk to show playing area

## How many can do it

Any number can be involved, but it is better if teams consist of more than 8 players.

## Where you can do it

It is best done outdoors in a large uncluttered space.

— CAN DO —

## How you can do it

Set up a pitch, similar to normal rounders, using four markers as the bases (or chalk small circles on ground), see below.

There is one bowler and you need four fielders, one on each of the bases, but otherwise, the fielders can stand anywhere.

The bowler rolls or kicks the ball to the 'batter' who simply kicks it out from the batting area, making sure it goes in front of them and travels at least 5 metres.

The batter is out if the ball is caught.

Once they have kicked, the batter is then required to run around the bases, trying to get to the fourth base before getting out; they can however, stop at any base at any time.

Runners are out if the football reaches the base they are running towards before they do, or if two runners find themselves at the same base.

Only the fielders on a base (the basekeepers) may run with the ball; everyone else must kick it

The batting team gets a run each time a runner reaches the fourth base. If they score a home run, that is get round in one go, they score double points.

When the batting team has 3 people out, the teams switch roles.

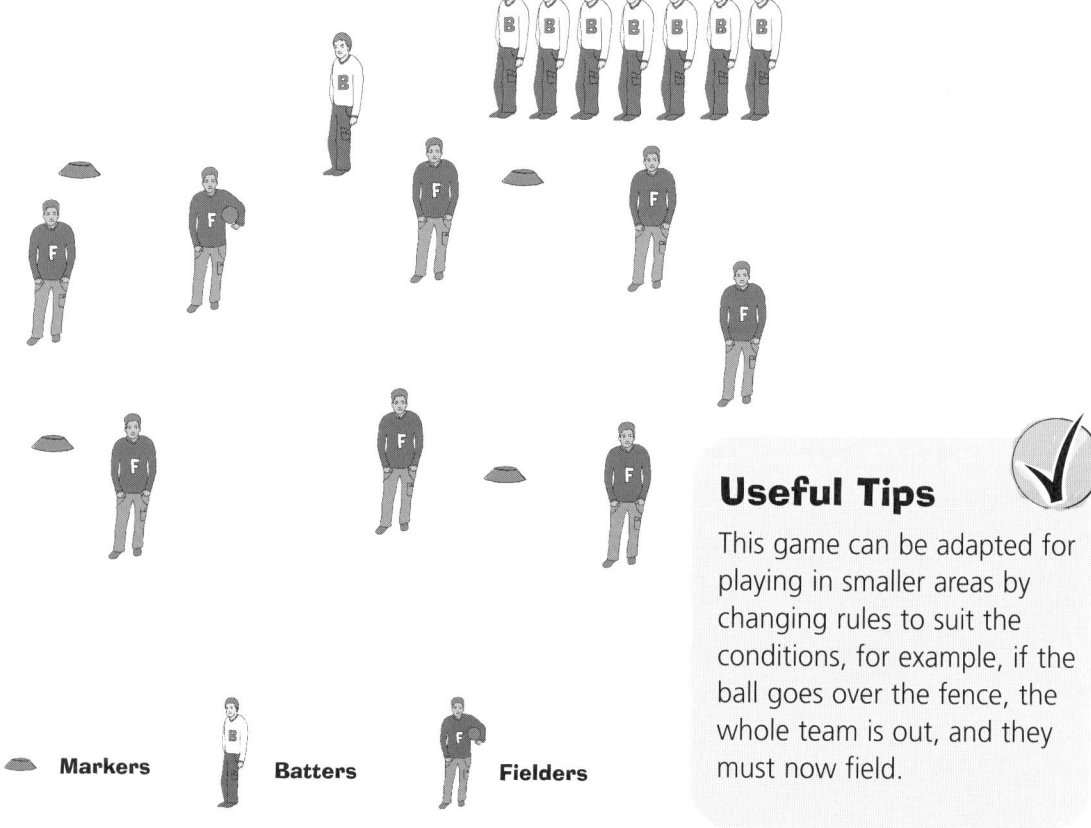

### Useful Tips

This game can be adapted for playing in smaller areas by changing rules to suit the conditions, for example, if the ball goes over the fence, the whole team is out, and they must now field.

COOL CREATIONS

## Spotlight—Play Safe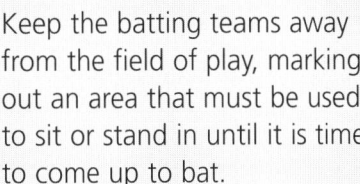

Here are some tips for playing in a safe environment, these should apply to all active sessions:

It's important to warm up to get the body ready for the activity. It helps to avoid injury and to get the mind focused on what you are about to do. Clubs will all have their favourite games for use as warm-ups

Everyone should wear appropriate clothing (comfortable and loose) for the activity session.

Wear appropriate footwear preferably trainers which provide a good grip and support. Ensure that laces are tied up properly—unfashionable perhaps, but much safer!

Jewellery and watches should be removed as they can cause an injury.

Make sure the playing surfaces are flat, free of obstacles and holes.

Do not leave equipment lying around—it is dangerous.

Be aware of your own safety, and that of others in the group, for example, not kicking the ball wildly when near other people.

## Safety Check

Keep the batting teams away from the field of play, marking out an area that must be used to sit or stand in until it is time to come up to bat.

For safety reasons, the fielders should be required to be at least 5 m away from the batter.

## Snapshot

The Children's Sports Centre run by Westminster Play Association use this type of game more often as an activity to either begin or end the morning or afternoon sessions as young people can join in or leave the game at any time, without it breaking down.

## What next?

Why not use a frisbee in place of a football, asking the group to throw it instead. The only difference would be that you would not have a bowler in the fielding team as the batter would start off by holding the frisbee.

For indoor use, or if your space is very small, why not get the group to play with a balloon, with the batter having to hit it out before running.

CAN DO

# Crossfire

## Why we like it

Using minimal materials, this game is fast and exciting and can be played indoors or outdoors, depending on the weather. It encourages and enables players to improve physical skills such as throwing accuracy, hand–eye co-ordination and balance. The game also promotes several social aspects including teamwork, patience and self-discipline. The idea for this game is very straightforward and can be altered in many ways to create new versions and different spins on what is already a very involving and stimulating game.

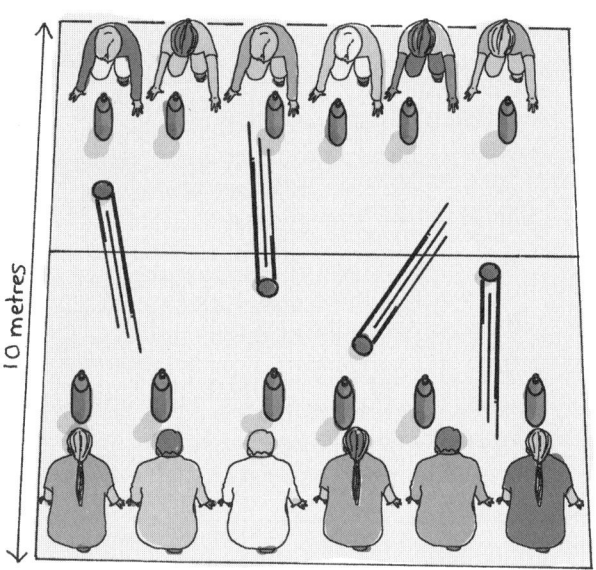

*Court dimensions and layout*

## What you might need

6 Frisbees
12 Plastic Bottles
(large fizzy drinks bottles would be ideal)
Cones or chalk to mark out court or playing area.

## How many can do it

Ideally the game would be played by 2 teams of 6, but could be adapted to cater for larger or smaller groups.

## Where you can do it

This game can be played indoors or outdoors, so is suitable for all year round enjoyment!

## COOL CREATIONS

### How you can do it

Lay out the court as on page 40.

The two teams should place their plastic bottles along their team line.

Each team starts with 3 frisbees.

Each player starts with 3 lives.

Standing behind their own bottles, the players must throw the frisbees at the the bottles of the opposing team.

When collecting frisbees to be thrown again, players may only pick those up which have come to rest in their own team's half of the court.

Players are not allowed to defend their bottles by stopping or catching the frisbees.

If your bottle is hit and knocked over you lose a life. You must reset your bottle before continuing.

When all 3 of your lives are lost, you must sit out of the game.

The team with the last player standing is the winner.

### Useful Tips

If played outside on a breezy day it is an idea to put a small amount of water into each bottle, just to give them a bit of extra stability and prevent them from being blown away.

### Safety Check

Players collecting fallen frisbees from the floor between the two team lines should remain alert at all times and avoid being caught up in the frisbee crossfire. An alternative method of collecting the frisbees would be to wait until all six discs have been thrown and then collect them all at once, however, employing this technique means that the game loses a great deal of it's frenetic excitement. The fact that the bottles are placed on the floor means that the frisbees will mostly be flying below waist height and the risk from being struck in the head is low.

### What next?

Why not try this game using a football (kicking) or tennis ball (throwing) instead of a frisbee.

You could also experiment with defenders who can be used to block the attacking projectiles. This might involve a catcher for the frisbee and tennis ball versions of the game and a goal keeper for the football version.

CAN DO

# Defender

## Why we like it

This is a very basic game and can be played by players of all abilities. It assists in the development of hand–eye co-ordination skills, balance and reflexes. The game also calls for an element of co-operation and strategy. It encourages the players to 'think' about their actions as well as giving them license to run, throw and hit the ball.

## What you might need

Tennis ball (or foam ball)
Cricket bat or tennis racquet.

## Where you can do it

This game can be played indoors or outdoors.

## How many can do it

There is no limit to how many people can play this game. If played outside, it is probably best to get as many people involved as possible.

COOL CREATIONS

## How you can do it

There is no set court or pitch for this game. It can be adapted to any available area.

The person selected to be the Defender needs to hold the bat or racquet in front of their shins.

The Defender must stand on a single spot for the duration of the game but is allowed to turn through 360° to face each thrower.

The other players must throw the tennis or foam ball at the Defender's shins.

The Defender must try to block the ball and prevent their shins being hit.

If the Defender successfully deflects the ball, the next thrower must throw the ball from the place it lands.

If the Defender fails to block the ball and the shins are hit, they must give up their bat to the successful thrower, who then becomes the Defender.

If the Defender hits the ball and it is caught before it bounces the Defender must give up their bat to the successful catcher.

### Useful Tips

Some players might want to use a tennis racquet instead of a cricket bat. The racquet is larger and therefore covers more of the shins. The use of a racquet would be particularly useful for players with 'less developed' reflexes.

### Safety Check

As long as the balls used in this game are relatively soft the players face no danger.

### What next?

If the Defender is very good it might be hard to get them out. If this happens introduce a second ball and let them try to defend against two throwers!

You could also have more than one Defender in the game. The introduction of additional balls or Defenders will require for the players to increase their concentration.

CAN DO

# Dodgeball Activities—3 games

## Why we like it

All these games are based on a form of dodgeball which is popular and fun to play, uses very little equipment and is ideal for playing both indoors and out. The activities help players to improve their throwing accuracy, anticipation, co-ordination and self-awareness. They are very good for encouraging team co-operation and decision-making.

Fig.1

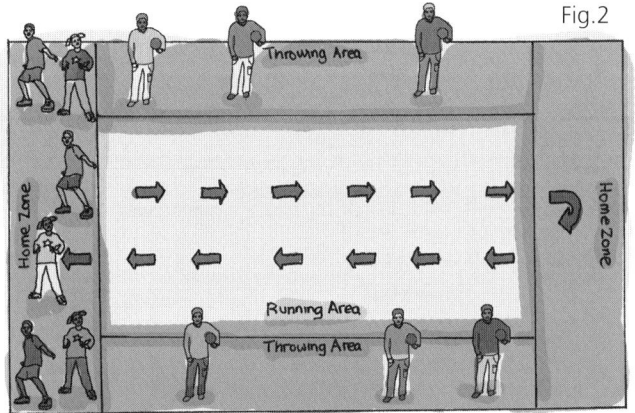

Fig.2

## How many can do it

These games are all very quick and simple to set up, can involve a large number of players and can be easily adapted to create new rules and formats—anything that keeps the ball moving.

## Where you can do it

The games can be played indoors or outside, although it can be easier to play where there is an enclosed space.

## What you might need

One or more large, soft balls (foam balls are ideal)

Cones or chalk to mark out playing area.

## COOL CREATIONS

## How you can do it

### Prisoner

Teams of 5+

Divide the playing area into 2 halves. In each half there needs to be another smaller area, the 'home zone ' (see Fig.1).

Divide the players into two teams, each standing in their own playing area.

Each team starts off with one or two balls. On the 'Start ' command, balls are thrown to hit opposing team members below the waist.

When players are hit (below the waist), they must move to stand in their home zone. They can then continue to attack the opposite team when in possession of a ball. Being hit above the waist or on the arms or hands does not count.

When attempting to avoid being hit, players are not allowed to go down onto the floor, but must try to catch the ball or deflect it with the arms or hands, or dodge as it comes towards them.

When collecting balls to throw at the other team, players can only pick up those balls in their own playing area or home zone, they cannot enter the opponent's area at any time.

Winners are the first team to get rid of all their opponents from the playing area.

### Home Run

Teams of 6+

Lay out the pitch as per the diagram (Fig.2)

One player from Team 2 runs from one home zone to the other and back again, trying to dodge being hit by a ball below the knee.

Team 1, who stand in the throwing area (see Fig.2), attempt to hit the running players below the knee with a number of soft balls.

If the running player in Team 2 gets home safely, they score a point, but if they are hit, they must leave the game. They can only remain in the home zone a given time, for example, 5 seconds, before starting their return run.

The game continues until all the running players are out, then the teams swap roles.

The team with the most points at the end of the game wins.

### Safety Check

Running players will need to be aware of where the balls are, so that they do not trip over them. Players collecting any balls from within the running area must take care not to collide or obstruct the running player.

### Safety Check

Make sure the balls are not so hard that they will hurt when they make contact—deflate them a little if necessary. Players need to ensure that they are throwing to hit the other team below the waist, not above. If a player deliberately throws to hit above the waist, they should be removed from the game straight away.
Introduce penalties if players continually go into their opponents' areas to collect the balls for example,. allow the opposing team to nominate a player to come back into their playing area.

CAN DO

## What next?

Why not have more than one player running at one time, for example, in pairs, although care will need to be taken so that there are no collisions. The game can also be made longer by having a set number of innings for each team, say five, carrying the scores over throughout. If players want to make the innings shorter, teams can always swap over once a given number of runners are out, for example, three.

### Jailbreak

Mark out a square approximately 10 metres x 10 metres (or use whatever room available) and mark a small circle in the middle (see Fig.3).

Select two or three players to act as prison guards. These players will be given a ball each to start with and must stand in the centre circle.

The remaining players will pose as escaping convicts and must stand in the corners of the square. They do not all have to stand in the same corner.

A direction for running must be agreed upon (clockwise or anti-clockwise—not diagonal).

When the command 'Jailbreak!' is given, the convicts will run to the next corner (in the agreed direction).

Whilst the convicts are running the prison guards will try to hit them (below the waist) with the ball.

The guards may go anywhere to retrieve their ball, but are only allowed to throw again when they have safely returned to the centre circle.

When convicts are hit they are 'captured' and must retire from the game.

The prison guard that captures the most convicts is the winner.

The last two or three convicts left 'on the run' will become the guards in the next game.

### Useful Tips

The larger the space available, the more Prison Guards you can use. If it becomes a recurring problem, prison guards who aim to hit convicts above the waist can be 'sacked from their job' and thrown in prison as a new convict.

### Safety Check

To avoid collisions, it is very important that all convicts run in the same direction. The Prison Guards must always aim to hit the convicts below the waist.

Fig.3

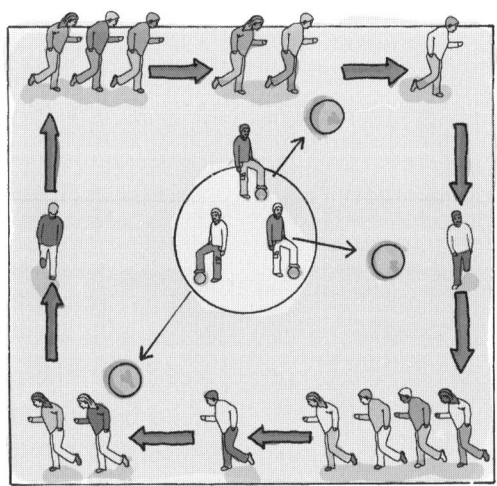

COOL CREATIONS

# Breakfast Club

**Scrumptious Smoothies, Mega Muesli and Yummy Banana and Honey Spread**

## Why we like it

Breakfast is often called the most important meal of the day! Having a good breakfast will help you stay healthy and boosts your concentration throughout the morning. Milk, cereals, fruit and nuts are all important sources of vitamins and minerals. Cereals and dried fruit can be good sources of fibre. These recipes need very little equipment and you don't even need a proper kitchen.

## What you might need

You'll need to be near an electricity power point and water for washing hands.

### Mega Muesli

This will make enough muesli for 8 people

100g porridge oats

8 tablespoons sultanas

100g ready to eat dried apricots, chopped

4 large oranges

4 eating apples or pears

Juice of 2 lemons

8 tablespoons clear (runny) honey

4 tablespoons mixed unsalted chopped nuts, for example, hazelnuts and almonds

8 tablespoons wheatgerm, plus extra for sprinkling

2 tablespoons sunflower seeds

2 tablespoons sesame seeds

Milk or Greek style yoghurt to serve

Large spoon and large bowl for mixing the muesli

Cereal bowls to serve in.

## How many can do it

1–6 depending on level of supervision available/needed.

## Where you can do it

Best done inside although breakfast can be eaten outside in nice weather!

## CAN DO

### How you can do it

Your need to make the Mega Muesli the night before you want to eat it!

**1.** Begin by reading through the instructions carefully. Clear a preparation area and make sure it is clean. Wash your hands thoroughly and put on an apron. Get all the ingredients and equipment you need so you won't have to hunt for anything half way through!

**2.** Put the oats and dried fruits in a large mixing bowl.

**3.** Add the grated zest of two of the oranges and the juice of all four.

**4.** Mix well, cover the bowl with cling film and leave to soak overnight.

**5.** Next morning, coarsely grate the apples or pears. Sprinkle with the lemon juice (it stops the fruit turning brown). Mix into the oats.

**6.** Stir in the honey, nuts, seeds and wheatgerm.

**7.** Divide into cereal bowls, sprinkle with wheatgerm and serve with milk or Greek-style yoghurt.

### Safety Check

This recipe contains nuts. For nut allergy sufferers, leave out the nuts and sesame seeds. Add extra fruit instead.

Be very careful when using sharp knives and electrical equipment, especially blenders! Never ever put your hand or a utensil into the blender when it is switched on.

### Useful Tips

The zest of an orange is the brightly coloured skin. Remove it using a medium grater - mind your fingers! Try not to grate any of the white pith under the skin, as this can taste bitter. You can use different fruits and use more or less honey, depending on how sweet you like the muesli.

COOL CREATIONS

## What you might need
### Scrumptious Smoothies
This will serve 8 people.

2 ripe mangoes, peeled, the stones removed and the flesh chopped

2 bananas, peeled and chopped

900ml milk

2 tablespoons honey

A blender

Small sharp knife for preparing the fruit

Tumblers

> **Useful Tips**
>
> You can used tinned mango instead of fresh, or use a different fruit. Strawberries might be nice!

## How you can do it
1. Put all the ingredients into a blender and blend until smooth. You may need to do this in two batches. If so, have a large jug to hand to put the blended smoothie into as you work.
2. Pour into tumblers and serve.


## What you might need
### Yummy Banana and Honey Spread
Makes enough for 8 large slices of bread.

50g of butter or spread, softened

2 tablespoons of honey

4 ripe bananas

8 slices of bread—your choice of brown or white

Wooden spoon to beat the spread

Fork to mash the bananas

Medium mixing bowl

Knife to cut the bread

> **Useful Tips**
>
> Ripe bananas are easier to mash and have more flavour.

## How you can do it
1. Put the butter or spread in the mixing bowl and beat with the wooden spoon until soft.
2. Peel the bananas, put them in the mixing bowl and mash them with a fork.
3. Add the honey to the bowl and mix everything thoroughly.
4. Spread generously onto the bread. Cut each slice into quarters and serve.

CAN DO

## Snapshot

'We weren't sure whether they would really go for the muesli ', said Sue, the co-ordinator of Early Starters Breakfast Club. 'It sounded a very adult taste. But we are part of a Healthy Living Centre so we were keen to try healthier options. We made up the muesli recipe as far as adding the juice the night before. We finished the recipe the next morning—it was great for giving the early arrivals something useful to do. We didn't use nuts or sesame seeds, just in case, and put extra dried fruit in. We used milk rather than yoghurt—it's cheaper. Some children needed a little extra sugar. We can't afford to use mangoes in the smoothies so we used extra bananas instead! It worked just as well. The children really enjoyed making the banana spread. They found it easier to butter the bread, rather than trying to mash the butter with the bananas and honey. We also used a spread rather than butter—its easier to use straight from the fridge and is a healthier option than butter. '

## Spotlight

Try to make breakfast a more interesting meal. If you don't like muesli, try adding a variety of fresh or dried fruit topping to a bowl of your favourite cereal. Have a glass of fruit juice instead of tea or coffee. Try different breads—especially wholegrain and wholemeal—as a way of increasing the amount of fibre you eat. Fibre is really important in making sure our digestive systems work properly and having adequate fibre in your diet is believed to help protect against certain cancers.

There is also a saying that you should 'breakfast like a king, lunch like a prince and dine like a pauper', which gives us a good idea of how we should spread our food intake throughout the day. Obviously, you need most energy, that is, food, during the day when you're active, and much less during the evening and night when you're relaxing or sleeping. People with diabetes need to spread their food intake through the day to ensure their body has a steady supply of blood sugar. Children with diabetes may need regular snacks to achieve this and an extra snack after strenuous activities. You can get advice on diabetes and appropriate diet from Diabetes UK, the new name of the British Diabetic Association. You can find them at *www.diabetes.org.uk*.

COOL CREATIONS

# Mega Meals

### Volcanic Chilli Con Carne (or Chilli Con Veggie)

## Why we like it

This meal is easy to prepare with minimum equipment. Because it uses lots of fresh ingredients it is nutritious, has little added salt or sugar, and if you serve with jacket potatoes, you're increasing the dietary fibre. It's also fairly cheap to make—important if you're catering for a group on a tight budget.

## How many can do it

1–6 depending on the space available and the amount of supervision required.

## Where you can do it

Anywhere that has access to water and where there are clean surfaces for preparing food. You'll need access to a hob (gas or electric) and somewhere to plug in a kettle for hot water for the stock.

## CAN DO

### What you might need

This chilli is medium hot—not that volcanic! You can reduce the spiciness by reducing the amount of dried chilli. You can also leave out the garlic and the green pepper if people don't like them.

Serves 6
450g minced beef or minced steak
2 medium onions, peeled and chopped
1 large clove of garlic, peeled and crushed
2 heaped tablespoons tomato puree
1 rounded tablespoon plain flour
Large tin red kidney beans, drained and rinsed
1 large green pepper, de-seeded and chopped
500ml hot stock (you can make this with beef stock cubes—follow the instructions on the stock cube packet).
1 level teaspoon chilli powder
A pinch of salt
A little oil for frying
Rice—follow quantities given on packet
Large pan with lid—a pan with a thick heavy base is best
Large pan to cook rice (if using)
Sharp knife for chopping onions and peppers
Garlic press
Teaspoon and tablespoon for measuring
Pint measuring jug for stock
Kettle for hot water for making stock
Tin opener for kidney beans tin
Sieve to rinse and drain beans and rice in
Wooden spoon for stirring
Apron.

For a vegetarian option or those who don't eat beef on religious grounds replace the mince with an equal amount of soya mince or use a selection of vegetables. You could use a mixture of potatoes, carrots, small white turnips or swede, peeled and chopped. Try adding broad, French or kidney beans or some chopped courgettes. If you use vegetables, reduce the cooking times to around 30–40 minutes. The vegetables need to be cooked until tender but not to a mush.

### Useful Tips

You can cook this in an oven if you prefer. When all the ingredients (except the pepper) are added, pour the chilli mix into an oven-proof casserole (with a lid) and cook in a pre-heated oven (Gas Mark 2, 300°F, 150°C). If using an oven, you'll need oven gloves to handle the casserole dish.

You can also make this using a microwave with variable power settings. Your microwave instruction book or a good microwave cookery book will tell you how to adapt cooking times. Remember to use only microwave safe dishes and utensils.

When chopping vegetables, try to get the pieces roughly the same size. This way they will cook in the same time.

COOL CREATIONS

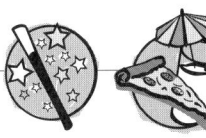

## How you can do it

**1.** Start by reading through the instructions, putting on an apron and washing your hands thoroughly.

**2.** Clear an area where you can prepare the meal. Make sure it is clean. Get all the equipment and ingredients ready so you won't need to go hunting for something half way through!

**3.** Heat a tablespoon of oil in the pan and cook the onion and garlic for about 5 minutes on a medium heat. Keep stirring and don't let the onion stick to the pan or burn.

**4.** Turn the heat to high, add the minced beef and brown it. Again, keep stirring. You want the meat to loose its pink colour but not to stick and burn.

**5.** Sprinkle in the plain flour and give everything a good stir. The flour will soak up the juices that have run out of the meat and will thicken the sauce.

**6.** Add the tomato puree to the meat mix. Stir thoroughly.

**7.** Add the hot stock. It's best to add it in three stages, stirring thoroughly after each addition. Be careful not to splash yourself.

**8.** Sprinkle in the chilli powder. Give the mixture a good stir. If you're not sure how hot the chilli will be, start by adding only a little chilli powder. You can always add more later on.

**9.** Add the red kidney beans and stir well.

**10.** Sprinkle in a pinch of salt. Give it all another good stir.

**11.** Bring the chilli con carne to a simmer (just bubbling), put the lid on the pan and cook for about $1\frac{1}{2}$ hours. Stir it occasionally, to make sure it isn't sticking to the pan.

**12.** Stir in the chopped green pepper. Cook for another 30 minutes.

**13.** Cook the rice following the instructions on the packet.

**14.** Taste test to see if the chilli con carne needs more salt or more chilli powder.

**15.** Serve with boiled rice or jacket potatoes (see 'What Next') or pitta bread.

## Safety Check

Always be very careful when using sharp knives. When chopping vegetables, it's important to use a chopping board on a firm surface.

Whenever you have handled raw onion, garlic, peppers or chilli powder, always wash your hands thoroughly and avoid rubbing your eyes!

Keep saucepan handles turned in so that people walking past can't knock them over.

## CAN DO

### Snapshot

Andy is the worker in charge of catering at Tigers, a breakfast, after school and holiday club. 'Food is really important here ', says Andy. 'We work in an area of incredible economic and social deprivation. The food the children get here may be the only nutritious food they get. We're lucky in that we have a good kitchen. The kids here take it in turns to work in small groups with me and a colleague in the kitchen. We have to stick to a budget but that's no bad thing as it means I have to develop cheap ideas and I can share them with parents. The chilli went down really well for lunch at the playscheme. We've served it with rice and did it again with jacket potatoes. We'll try it for tea at the after school club, but as we don't have much time then we'll make the chilli the day before and give it a mashed potato topping, like a shepherds pie but with more bite! '

### What next?

This would make a nice spicy topping for jacket potatoes. Here's how to cook them.

Wash each potato thoroughly. Dry them on kitchen roll or a tea towel. Using a fork, carefully prick each potato all over—this stops the potatoes exploding when you cook them!

If you have an oven, heat it to 400°F, 200°C or Gas Mark 6. Put the potatoes in the oven—the centre shelf will be fine. Bake them for $1-1\frac{1}{2}$ hours, depending on how large they are. You can tell if they're cooked because they'll feel soft when squeezed gently —use oven gloves to do this though! You can speed up the cooking time by pushing (carefully) a metal skewer through each potato. The metal conducts heat more quickly to the centre of the spud. Don't do this if you're using a microwave—microwaves and metal don't mix!

If you are using a microwave, cook the potatoes on high. For a potato weighing 175g, the cooking times are 5–6 minutes for one potato; 8-10 minutes for two; 9–12 minutes for three and 10–15 minutes for four. You may find it helpful to turn the potatoes over halfway through the cooking time.

COOL CREATIONS

## Cool Cocktails

**Fabulous Fruit Cocktails, Marvelous Milk Shakes and Fizzy Floats**

### Why we like them

Fruit cocktails are a healthy alternative to fizzy drinks and are a great tasting way to eat more fruit. We should all try to eat (or drink!) five portions of fresh fruit or vegetables each day to stay healthy. You can be as creative and experimental as you like mixing different juices—everyone will have their own favourite combination. Milk is a great source of calcium—we all need this for strong teeth and bones. Fizzy Floats are so easy, and cheap to make and don't require any special equipment!

### What you might need
**Fabulous Fruit Cocktails**

Makes 10–12 drinks

3 x 1 litre cartons of pure fruit juice—orange, pineapple and peach work well, or try cranberry with orange—chilled

Variety of fresh fruit or tinned fruit with the juice drained off, (tinned pineapple and mango work well, choose fruit in juice rather than fruit in syrup.)

Ice cubes or crushed ice

Cold water or fizzy mineral water (optional)

Tumblers which hold about 300ml of liquid

Large jug for mixing juice in and large spoon for stirring

Sharp knives to prepare fruit

Chopping board(s)

Kitchen scissors (to open juice cartons) and can opener (if using tinned fruit)

Cocktail sticks, umbrellas and straws

Aprons.

### How many can do it

1–6 depending on preparation space available and level of supervision required.

### Where you can do it

Best done indoors to avoid attracting wasps and other insects! You don't need a kitchen, as long as there are tables you can work at, running water for washing and a freezer nearby to keep the ice cream and ice cubes. For Marvelous Milk Shakes you'll need a power supply nearby if you want to use a blender or electric whisk.

CAN DO

## How you can do it

**1.** Start by reading through the instructions, putting on an apron and washing your hands thoroughly.

**2.** Clear an area where you can prepare the drinks. Make sure it is clean. Get all the equipment and ingredients ready so you won't need to go hunting for something half way through!

**3.** Begin by preparing the fruit kebabs.

**4.** If using fresh fruit, wash it carefully under cold running water.

**5.** If necessary, use a small sharp knife to peel the fruit and remove the core or stones. Be careful using sharp knives and make sure your chopping board is on a firm, level surface.

**6.** Cut the fruit into attractive bite size shapes.

**7.** Thread different types of fruit onto the cocktail sticks. Set aside while you make the drinks.

**8.** Shake the cartons of juice to make sure the contents are well mixed. Taking care when opening the cartons to make sure juice doesn't spurt everywhere.

**9.** Mix equal quantities of each juice together in a large jug. Give it a good stir with a large spoon.

**10.** Tip ice cubes or crushed ice into each tumbler—you can add as much or as little as you want but the more ice you put in the less room there'll be for juice!

**11.** Pour the juice mix into the tumbler.

**12.** Decorate with drinking straws and cocktail umbrellas. Rest a fruit cocktail stick across the top of each tumbler. Serve while still chilled.

## What you might need
### Marvelous Milk Shakes

Chilled fresh milk - about 300ml per person
Flavoured syrups suitable for milkshakes, available at the supermarket
Spoons for measuring and stirring
Tumblers which hold about 300ml of liquid
Drinking straws
Large jug for mixing the milk shakes
Hand or electric whisk or a blender
Aprons.

## How you can do it

**1.** Following the instructions on the bottle, pour the recommended quantity of syrup into a large jug.

**2.** Add cold milk according to the instructions on the syrup bottle. (If the flavour is too strong, you can add extra milk.)

**3.** Whisk thoroughly with a hand whisk or electric mixer until the syrup is well mixed and the drink is frothy. If you use a blender pour the syrup and milk into the jug of the blender.

**4.** Pour into tumblers and add a drinking straw.

**5.** Drink while still chilled.

**6.** Decorate fruit flavour drinks with pieces of fruit slotted on the rim of the tumbler. Sprinkle crumbled chocolate flake or chocolate powder on top of chocolate milkshakes.

**7.** Experiment with coffee flavour by mixing one level teaspoon of instant coffee per drink in a little hot water until dissolved. Allow to cool then mix with cold milk as above. Top with chocolate powder, crumbled flake or chocolate sprinkles.

## Safety Check

Always be very careful when using sharp knives. If serving the drinks to young children, leave out the ice as young children can easily choke on small objects. Unbreakable tumblers are safer than glass ones.

COOL CREATIONS

## What you might need

### Fizzy Floats

Big bottles of fizzy drinks—lemonade, cherryade, limeade, for example. A two litre bottle of lemonade will make eight drinks.

Tub of ice cream—flavour of your choice, but vanilla works with everything! A two litre tub of ice cream will be enough for 20 drinks.

Spoon or ice cream scoop

Tumblers which hold about 300ml of liquid

Drinking straws

Aprons.

## How you can do it

Pour the fizzy drink into tumblers, leaving a gap of about 5cms to the top of the tumbler.

Top each tumbler with a scoop of ice cream.

Add a drinking straw and serve immediately.

## Snapshot

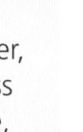

The Zoo is an after school club based at a sports centre. 'We loved the cocktails, ' said the Playleader, Helen. 'We don't have a proper kitchen, just access to a staff rest room. It only has a microwave, kettle, sink and fridge, so we can't do much cookery. The cocktails made a super treat at our end of term party. Some people preferred the fresh fruit juice watered down—we used tap water as they weren't too keen on fizzy mineral water because its not sweet like lemonade! One of the staff brought in her liquidiser to mix the milk shakes. It's made us think much more creatively about what cookery we can try. It also led onto a discussion about where all the different fruits came from and what they grew on. We got our atlas out and started looking up the different countries. Next term we plan to develop this interest so that all of us can learn a lot more about food from around the world—and enjoy eating some of it.'

## What next?

These extra special drinks could be part of a celebration party. Or you could sell them at summer fundraising events. Make sure you charge enough to cover the cost of the ingredients and to make a profit.

## Useful Tips

If you find pure juices are too strong for your liking, or to make juice go further, mix juice with an equal quantity of water. Fizzy mineral water will give a tingle to the drink. For a sweeter drink, mix juice with an equal quantity of lemonade.

In summer, supermarkets have good offers on packs of peaches and nectarines. One pack of each and a melon or box of strawberries will be enough fruit to decorate about 30 cocktails.

You could also try making ice cubes from fruit juice or freezing pieces of fruit into ice cubes.

CAN DO

# Snack Attack

### Pepperoni Pizza Toasties and Muesli Flapjack Snackbars

## Why we like them

These snacks are quick and easy to make and don't need lots of equipment or a state-of-the-art kitchen—only a hob and a grill. They have little added salt or sugar, and lots of fresh ingredients so they're quite healthy.

## How many can do it

1–6, depending on the size of the preparation area and the level of supervision required.

## Where you can do it

Anywhere where there is a suitable, clean preparation area, with access to water for washing hands. You'll need a hob (gas or electric) and a grill for the pizzas and a microwave oven for the flapjack snack bars.

## Useful Tips

Bread that is a day or two old slices better than new baked bread.
For vegetarians, leave out any meat and animal products. Choose a cheese suitable for vegetarians and use lots of sliced red onion, chopped sweet peppers, ripe tomatoes, mushrooms and sweetcorn. Fresh herbs—particularly basil—will add flavour and colour.

## What you might need

### Pepperoni Pizza Toasties

Makes 10 slices

1 large bread loaf, unsliced—your choice of white or brown

1 x 400g can chopped tomatoes in juice

1 medium onion, peeled and chopped but still quite chunky

1 tablespoon tomato puree

1 tablespoon olive oil

Large pinch dried mixed herbs

60 thin slices of pepperoni—you'll want about 6 slices per toastie

250g grated cheese—your choice. A mature cheddar has lots of flavour. Mozarella is the traditional pizza cheese. Try a mix of both.

Bread knife, sharp knife for chopping onion

Chopping board

Tablespoons for measuring

Tin opener

Saucepan.

COOL CREATIONS

## Useful Tips

You can vary the toppings as much as you like. Try ham and pineapple chunks or flakes of tuna with sweetcorn. Grilled chopped bacon and fried mushrooms would be tasty.

## How you can do it

1. Start by reading through the instructions, putting on an apron and washing your hands thoroughly.

2. Clear an area where you can prepare the soup. Make sure it is clean. Get all the equipment and ingredients ready so you won't need to go hunting for something half way through!

3. Heat the oil in the saucepan over a medium heat. Add the onions and cook for 5 minutes. Keep stirring the pan and don't let the onions burn.

4. Add the tomato puree, tinned tomatoes and mixed herbs. Simmer gently (just bubbling) for about 20 minutes until you have a thickish sauce. You'll need to stir the sauce from time to time, to stop it sticking and burning. Add salt, pepper and sugar to taste—tomatoes often need a little sugar to bring out the flavour.

5. Cut the bread loaf into 1–1½ cm thick slices. Toast them under the grill or in a toaster.

6. Spread a dollop of the sauce on each slice. Add slices of pepperoni to each and top with grated cheese. Put under a hot grill until the cheese has melted.

7. Cut in half and serve.

## Safety Check

Always be careful when using sharp knives to chop vegetables. Make sure saucepan handles are turned inwards so that pans cannot be easily knocked off the hob.

## Snapshot

Rascals is an after school club based in a school. Sally is the co-ordinator. 'We only have access to a kitchen used by staff but the children aren't allowed in. The children did the preparation and then we whisked the toasties off to finish under the grill. We made the tomato sauce in advance and heated it up at the club. The snack bars were even better because we brought the microwave into the club room, so the children could do everything. This has really made us think about how we can adapt recipes to our limited facilities. It was also interesting to see how the older children supervised and helped the younger ones and the fascination they developed for weights and measures. 150g of margarine seems a much smaller quantity than 150g of porridge oats! As a result we created a guess and check game where you have to guess the weight, length or height of an object and then check it by weighing or measuring.'

## CAN DO

### What you might need
**Museli Flapjack Snackbars**

Makes 12 bars

150g butter or margarine

75g soft brown sugar

150g porridge oats

50g sunflower seeds

50g chopped mixed nuts

50g raisins or sultanas

A large microwave safe bowl

Wooden spoon for mixing and flattening

A shallow round microwave safe dish, about 20–21cm in diameter

A knife to slice the bars

A fork

### How you can do it

**1.** Start by reading through the instructions, putting on an apron and washing your hands thoroughly.

**2.** Clear an area where you can prepare the snackbars. Make sure it is clean. Get all the equipment and ingredients ready so you won't need to go hunting for something half way through!

**3.** Put the butter or margarine in the bowl and cook on high for 2 minutes until melted.

**4.** Add all the other ingredients and mix thoroughly.

**5.** Tip into the shallow dish and press down well. Cook in the microwave on high for 5 minutes.

**6.** The snackbars will be very uneven. Press them down again with the back of a fork. Slice into twelve pieces. Leave to cool and harden before eating.

### Safety Check
Be careful when lifting out the bowl of melted butter. The liquid will be very hot. These snackbars contain nuts. For nut allergy sufferers, omit the nuts and the sesame seeds and increase the quantity of sunflower seeds, oats and dried fruit.

### Spotlight
If you have to provide food for people it is important to know if any have allergies to certain foods. In an organised setting records of allergies must be kept. If you are entertaining friends' children it is a good idea to ask parents or carers about any allergies otherwise they may assume you know. Peanut and tree nut allergies are high profile at present because they seem to be on the increase and can in rare cases lead to anaphylactic shock which can be fatal. People who are intolerant to nuts may also react to sesame seeds. The Nut Allergy Network has a web site full of helpful information at *www.nutallergy.net*.

You may also come across gluten intolerance. Gluten is a substance found in wheat. People who are intolerant to gluten need to remove wheat products from their diet or replace them with gluten free products. For more information try *www.gluten-free.co.uk*.

### Useful Tips
In a microwave, food cooks more evenly in round dishes than square ones. With square dishes, the corners tend to get over-cooked. That's why the snackbars are cooked in a round dish.

### What next?
You could try varying the dried fruit. Try chopped ready to eat dried apricots or papaya for a more exotic touch. Use this as an opportunity to talk about food from around the world.

COOL CREATIONS

# Party Pieces

### Minty Lamb Burgers and Mandarin Foam

## Why we like them

These are cheap and cheerful recipes for a celebration meal—perhaps a barbecue to celebrate a birthday or the end of the holiday playscheme!

## What you might need

### Minty Lamb Burgers

Makes 16 burgers

1kg minced lamb (if using frozen mince, allow to defrost thoroughly before using)

150g breadcrumbs made from an old bread loaf

2 onions, peeled and finely chopped

6 tablespoons chopped mint

2 medium eggs, beaten together in a small bowl

1 tablespoon orange juice

Salt and pepper

A little oil for cooking

A large bowl to mix the ingredients

Sharp knife to chop mint and onions with

Tablespoons for measuring

Small bowl for eggs

Fork to beat eggs

Aprons.

## How many can do it

1–6, depending on the size of the preparation area and the level of supervision required.

## Where you can do it

Anywhere where you can make a clean preparation area and where there is water for washing hands—very important when handling raw meat and eggs which can carry food poisoning bacteria.

## Useful Tips

Fresh herbs like mint, parsley and basil are readily available in supermarkets, but it's easy and fun to grow your own in plant pots on window ledges. This could be the start of a gardening project.

— CAN DO —

## How you can do it

1. Start by reading through the instructions, putting on an apron and washing your hands thoroughly.

2. Clear an area where you can prepare the meals. Make sure it is clean. Get all the equipment and ingredients ready so you won't need to go hunting for something half way through!

3. Mix all the ingredients together thoroughly in a large mixing bowl.

4. Divide into 16 equal amounts and shape into burgers.

5. Lightly brush each burger with oil. Grill, fry or barbecue for 3-4 minutes each side, or until cooked through.

6. Serve in burger buns with salad.

7. For a vegetarian version use vegemince to replace the lamb and follow the instructions on the packet

### What next?

Try adding finely chopped ready to eat dried apricots or finely chopped red peppers to the burger mix to give a mediterranean taste.

## Safety Check

Follow basic health and safety guidance. You must wash your hands as soon as you've shaped the burgers and make sure the burgers are cooked through. Raw meat and eggs can harbour food poisoning bacteria.

If you need to store them before cooking, keep them, covered, in a fridge. Remember, raw meat should always be stored below cooked meat.

Care should always be taken when using sharp knives and electrical equipment.

Be careful not to cut yourself on the tin cans.

## What you might need
### Mandarin Foam

Serves 8

1 x 410g tin evaporated milk, well chilled (leave in fridge overnight)
1 x 135g packet mandarin jelly
1 small tin mandarin segments Large bowl
Spoon for stirring
Knife to chop mandarins
Electric whisk or hand whisk
Tin opener
Measuring jug
Kettle.

## How many can do it

1–6, depending on size of preparation area and level of supervision required.

## Where you can do it

Anywhere with water for washing hands and where you can set up a clean preparation area. You'll need access to a fridge, and somewhere to plug in an electric whisk, if using, and a kettle.

COOL CREATIONS

## How you can do it

1. Start by reading through the instructions, putting on an apron and washing your hands thoroughly.

2. Clear an area where you can prepare the meals. Make sure it is clean. Get all the equipment and ingredients ready so you won't need to go hunting for something half way through!

3. Make up the jelly in a measuring jug, according to the instructions on the packet. Leave to cool, but not set.

4. Tip the evaporated milk into the large bowl. Whisk until beginning to foam. Pour in the jelly in a steady stream, whisking all the time. Whisk until you have a thick foam. Add the chopped up manadarins and whisk some more.

5. Leave to set in a fridge.

6. Serve with ice cream or squirty (canned) cream.

### Useful Tips

You can vary the flavour of the jelly and fruit.

### What next?

You could pour the foam into a jelly mould then leave to set in the fridge. Decorate with cream and fruit to make a stunning centre piece to a party table. Pour into individual serving dishes before leaving to set.

## Spotlight

A barbecue is just one way of cooking. You might like to research different ways of cooking in different parts of the world or in different ages. Can you imagine what it would really be like to cook over an open fire—the smoke, smell, overdone on the outside and undercooked in the middle, and the huge task of constantly collecting firewood. How do the ovens available now differ from the equipment your grandparents and great grandparents had? How has diet changed over the years? What would it be like to live with rationing—a time, when ironically many people were at their healthiest!

Barbecues can potentially cause food poisoning because they often don't get hot enough to cook the food right through. If you have responsibility for catering, you should study for a Food Handling Certificate. A one day course may be all you need, and it will give you an understanding of food poisoning bacteria, where they live, how they spread, how to destroy them, and how to adopt basic good hygiene practice in the workplace and at home. Contact your local college of further education for details of courses.

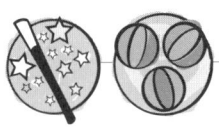

CAN DO

## Great Balls of Beans—Making Juggling Balls

### Why we like it

Having your own juggling balls makes it easier to learn to juggle. The balls will be filled with beans so that they fit into your hand perfectly. You can make them in lots of different materials so that you can have your very own design for your personal set of juggling balls.

Pattern cutting and sewing are great skills to learn or practice and will come in useful time and time again. This is a nice calming activity. If you want to get juggling as quickly as possible you may like to try the balloon balls suggestion under 'Useful Tips' in this section.

### What you might need

Material: a 30 cm square of your chosen materials for 3 balls. Cotton, jersey or towelling is best, but any fabric that you can sew will do.

Cutting pattern (see Fig.1)

Needles

Thread

Scissors

Card (for pattern)

Funnel

Pencil (for marking and stuffing)

Beans—mung beans or pulses of a similar size.

### How many can do it

This is an ideal group activity. You can run this activity with as many in the group as you have materials for.

### Where you can do it

Inside around a table is best. There is room for you to spread out and this also provides a confined space to chase around after those wayward beans.

COOL CREATIONS

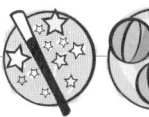

## How you can do it

**1.** Make a template for your pattern by copying, marking and cutting out the shape in Fig.1. You may find it easier to photocopy the figure and stick it onto the card and then cut around it.

**2.** Now place your material on a smooth flat surface with the design side down. Mark around the template onto the fabric until you have as many pieces marked out as you want. Remember you will need 4 pieces for each ball that you want to make. 12 pieces will make a set of three juggling balls.

**3.** Cut out the shapes and mark each one as shown in Fig.2, that is, A at the top, B at the bottom, C on the left and D on the right. This will make joining up the pieces easier. Now mark a line approximately 0.5 cm from the edge all the way round—this line will show you where to stitch.

**4.** Now you can start to join up the pieces of fabric to make your juggling balls. Take two pieces of fabric and put them together with the design facing each other. Make sure that both A's are at the top. Now sew down your stitch guide on the left hand side from A down to B following the guide line—see Fig.2, make your stitches small and tight so that no beans can escape. Sew all of the remaining pieces together into pairs.

**5.** Take two of the pairs that you have sewn together making sure that the A's are at the top. Holding the pairs together with the design on the inside sew the two pairs together down one side, see Fig.3. Match up your remaining pairs and sew them likewise.

**6.** Take one of your joined sets of pairs and sew part down from A and part way up from B making sure that you leave a whole big enough to push all of the fabric through, see Fig.4.

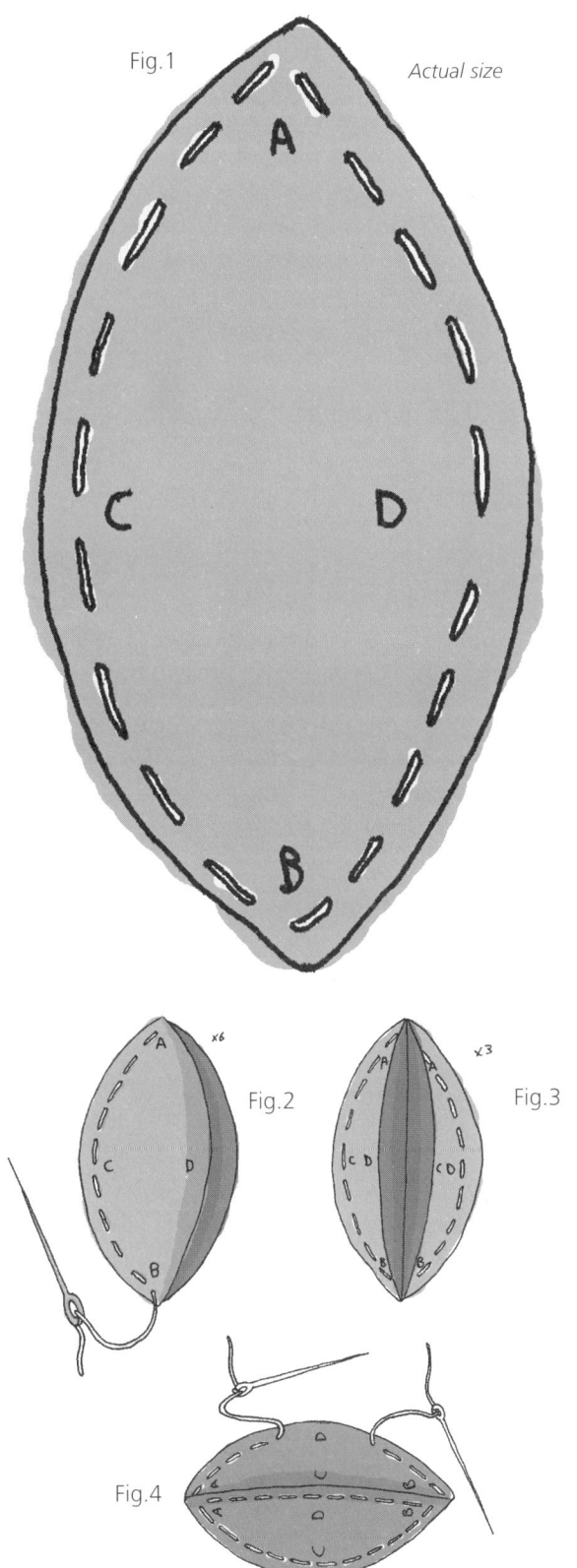

Fig.1 — Actual size

Fig.2  Fig.3  Fig.4

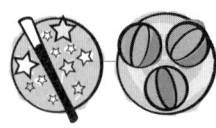

CAN DO

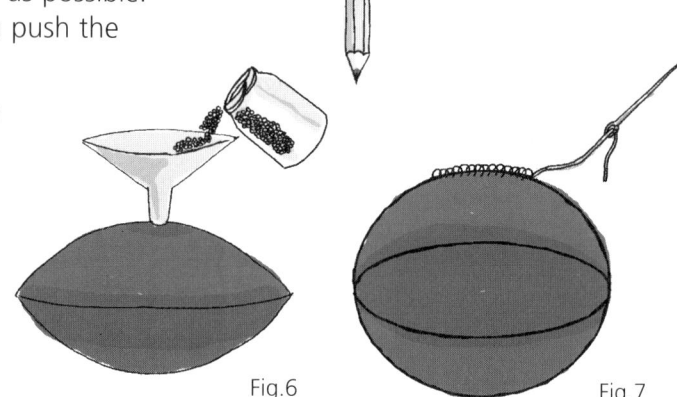

Fig.5

Fig.6

Fig.7

7. Now carefully push all of the fabric through the hole you have left so that the design is now on the outside, see Fig.5 - you might find the pencil handy to help the fabric through.

8. Insert the funnel and pour in your beans, see Fig.6—you want as many beans in there as possible. You can use the pencil to make sure you push the beans into all the gaps.

9. Now carefully sew up the hole with small stitches and make your last knot, see Fig.7. You now have your very own juggling ball—two more to go and you'll be ready to Juggle!

## Useful Tips

If you want to make juggling balls more easily or with those who don't want to sew, then why not try balloon balls. You'll need 6 balloons for each set of 3 balls, some beans, a funnel and a pair of scissors. Fill one balloon with beans—as many as you can so it's a good size to fit in your hand. Now tie the end and cut of the excess. Cut off the neck of the second balloon and cut out two more round holes from elsewhere on the balloon. Now stretch the second balloon over the first making sure that the knot in the first balloon is hidden under the second balloon—instant juggling balls! These balls will not last as long as the fabric one's but if you want to start your juggling activity sooner then this is a good way to get started.

## What next?

Design your own fabric and then make it into balls

Make your juggling balls in all sorts of shapes. From books to bunnies, pompoms to penguins the list is just about endless. Try to make your designs as creative as you can whilst keeping the size and overall shape comfortable to hold and catch. Keep your patterns simple and experiment—you may find inspiration and ideas in pattern books for soft toys. Try your local library or second hand book shop.

Learn to juggle—see What's Round Goes Round, on page 67.

COOL CREATIONS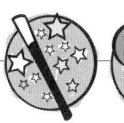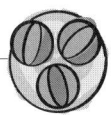

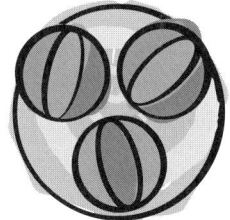

# What's Round Goes Round—How to Juggle

## Why we like it

From the time of court jesters to the present day people have always marvelled at those who can keep a number of objects in the air at the same time. This is a great way to improve hand–eye co-ordination, and can improve your ability in all sorts of activities, hobbies and sports. It's also a great activity in itself, and you can carry juggling balls around with you everywhere and practice when you like. Once you have mastered the basics you can juggle just about anything, Try making your own juggling balls for that personal touch, see Great Balls of Beans on page 64.

## What you might need

Three balls or bean bags for each person taking part—although when you are starting you will only need one or two balls each.

## How many can do it

There is no optimum number. When starting it may be easier to try it out in a group and learn from each other. Once you have got the basics you can practice just about anywhere, either on your own or in a group.

## Where can you do it

Ideally out doors on a dry, windless day but equally good inside with a high ceiling and enough space to move around. Gyms or halls are excellent spaces to learn to juggle if you have access to one.

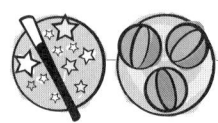

CAN DO

## How to do it?

1.  There are lots of different ways to juggle (and lots of things to juggle). The cascade is the easiest pattern to learn so we will start there. The cascade involves throwing objects into the air with both hands, in a criss cross pattern in front of you.

2.  To get started find a space of your own and put a ball in your right hand and throw it in an arc to your left hand, see Fig.1. If you catch it—great—throw the ball back to your right hand in the same arc. If you miss it—don't worry, pick it up and throw it in an arc to your right hand from your left. It is more important that the ball flies in a nice smooth arc than you catch it at this stage. Try to keep the height of the arc the same on each throw—just above head height is great. Congratulations! You are now a one ball juggler.

3.  Now take two balls—one in each hand. Start in the same way by throwing the ball in your right hand in an arc to your left hand. Once this ball reaches the middle of its arc throw the ball in your left hand in an arc to your right hand, see Fig.2. Don't worry about catching them at first, just concentrate on making them travel in an arc at about the same height. Once you are comfortable with throwing, try to catch one ball each time and work up to catching both.

You may find that you throw one ball in an arc and the other ball gets passed directly from one hand to the other rather than thrown, see Fig.3. If this happens try starting with the other hand.

You are now a two ball juggler—Well Done!

4.  Now using three balls. Take two balls in your right hand and one in your left. Start by throwing the first ball in your right hand in an arc to your left. When this ball reaches the middle of its arc throw the ball in your left hand in an arc to your right hand. Once this ball reaches the middle of its arc throw the second ball in your right hand in an arc to your left hand, see Fig.4.

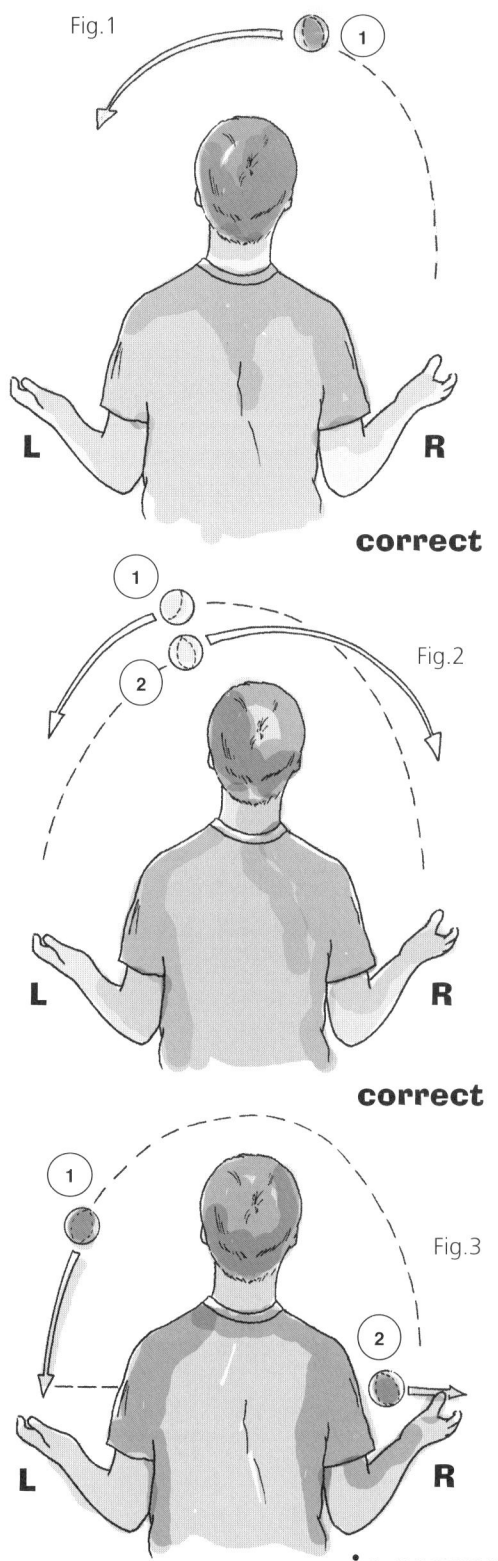

COOL CREATIONS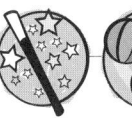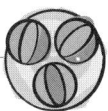

**5.** Do not attempt to catch any of the balls at first. Concentrate on the height of the arc and on getting a rhythm going between each hand, this will help when you start to juggle all three for longer periods. You can use the sound of the balls hitting the floor to gauge your rhythm.

**6.** When you feel comfortable throwing all three balls in succession and you have a good even arc on your throws try catching the first ball you throw. Practise until you are catching all three. At this stage, all you need to do is to start throwing the balls that you catch. Try catching and re-throwing the first ball and practise until you can throw and catch and re-throw all three.

You are now a fully-fledged juggler!

**7.** Keep practising, build up the number of throws you can do before you drop a ball. You could keep records of everyone's progress on a wall chart in your club.

## Useful Tips

Always look straight ahead and not at your hands. Throw the balls slightly higher—it will give you more time to react.

If you find yourself throwing the balls forward rather than straight up, juggle with a wall in front of you, so the balls will bounce of the wall and back into your hand. It will also save you from running a lot!

Use bean bags or your own home-made juggling balls that will stay in your hand more easily than harder balls and you'll be likely to catch and hold onto them.

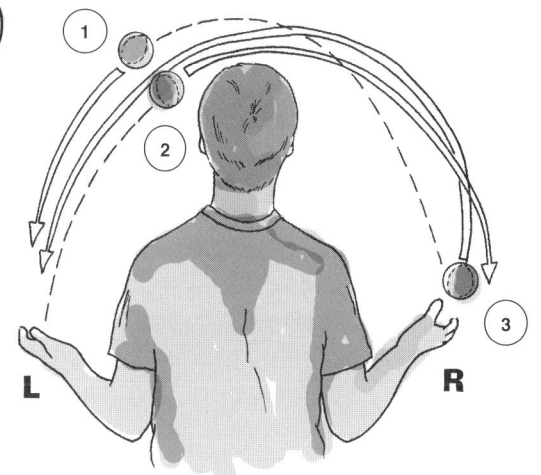

**correct**  Fig 4

## What next?

Find books in the library to explore other juggling patterns and tricks.

Make your own, personalised juggling balls, see Great Balls of Beans on page 64.

Teach your friends to juggle. Once you have mastered the art of juggling you can help your friends to learn by making a juggling duo. You and a friend stand side by side with an arm around each others shoulders. You will be the right hand and they will be the left. Start as you did when you started with one ball and work up to throwing and catching all three. This method will help your friends to learn and improve your own juggling at the same time as you try to catch their wayward throws and keep the juggling going.

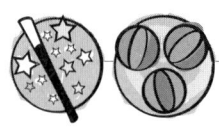

CAN DO

# Walk Tall—Making Stilts

## Why we like it

Making your own stilts is a great way to learn to stilt walk and will add to the sense of achievement when you go off on a walk as a giant, as part of a performance or just for show. This activity involves learning or practising practical skills of sawing and drilling. This is also a great activity for working on co-operation and working in pairs. Making stilts can provide the opportunity to put something back into your club by making equipment that you will use but that will be used by others who attend your club for years to come.

## What you might need

For each pair of stilts:

Wood

1.30 m length of 5 cm x 5 cm (cut into two 65 cm lengths)

30 cm length of 10 cm x 5 cm (cut into two 15 cm lengths)

20 cm square of 2.5 cm thick ply board (cut into two 20 cm x 10 cm pieces)

Four straps with buckles—old belts are particularly good

An old bicycle tyre—cut out the tread and cut strips—2 x 7 cm and 2 x 25 cm

4 x 12.5 cm long 0.65 cm bolts with wing nuts

8 x No 10 wood screws 6.5 cm long

4 x No 6 wood screws 2.5 cm long

60 cm x 30 cm piece of soft foam

Nails

Drill

0.5 cm and 1.25 cm wood drill bits

Wood Saw—or get the wood yard to cut the wood to size

Hammer

Protective safety glasses

Screw Driver

Spanner

Tape

Stanley knife

Work bench.

## How many can do it

2 to a small group. Working in pairs works well with this activity either each working on one stilt or sharing the work on both. Groups work well too, group size will depend on the number of stilts to be made.

## Where can you do it

Inside or outside as long as there is access to the tools you need and a work bench.

COOL CREATIONS

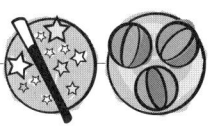

## How you can do it

**1.** Cut the wood into the desired sizes or get your wood yard or resource centre to do it for you.

**2.** Carefully measure out and mark all holes to be drilled before drilling the desired holes in your wood see Fig.1.

**3.** For each 60 cm lengths of 5 cm x 5 cm, draw a line down the centre of the length—top to bottom. Measure up 15 cm from the bottom and make a mark across the centre line. Using this point as a reference mark 5 cm and 10 cm above this mark, so that you have 3 marks on each length, one at 15 cm from the bottom, one at 20 cm and one at 25 cm. Drill holes through using the 1.25 cm drill bit.

**4.** Take each 20 cm x 10 cm piece of 2.5 cm thick ply board - On one long edge mark a rectangle 10 cm x 5 cm against the edge and 5 cm from either end. Mark drill holes at each corner within this rectangle half an inch from each edge. Drill holes using a 0.5 cm drill bit to accommodate your 6.5 cm wood screws.

**5.** Take each 15 cm length of 10 cm x 5 cm. On the 15 cm x 10 cm side draw a line dividing the longest side in two (that is, 7.5 cm from each end). Mark drill holes across this line 2.5 cm from the top and bottom—the centre of the drill holes should be exactly 5 cm apart so that they match perfectly match the holes you have already drilled in the 5 cm x 5 cm, see Fig.1. Drill holes through using the 1.25 cm drill bit.

**6.** Now use the holes drilled into the 20 cm x 10 cm board to mark the drill holes in the top of this piece of wood by placing the board on top of the 10 cm x 5 cm. Make sure that the 10 cm x 5 cm fits exactly into the rectangle you drew on the 20 cm x 10 cm board. Now drill these holes using the 0.5 cm sized drill bit to a depth of about 2 cm.

**7.** Attach the 20 cm x 10 cm board to the 10 cm x 5 cm using the 6.5 cm screws, see Fig.1. This is the foot platform. Now nail the 25 cm section of tyre to the front end of the platform 2.5 cm back from the end—this will hold the front of the stilt walker's foot straight on the platform.

**8.** Nail the 7.5 cm sections of tyre to the bottom of each length of 5 cm x 5 cm making sure that the nails go into the side of the wood and not the bottom—this will give your stilts a good grip.

**9.** Screw two straps to the top of each stilt— one at 5 cm from the top and one at 15 cm from the top.

**10.** Using the bolts and wing nuts, attach the foot platform to the 5 cm length of 5 cm x 5 cm using the lowest two holes. Make sure that the foot platform is attached to the opposite side to the straps, see Fig.1.

**11.** Make sure that all of your screws are tight and that you have nailed all of the pieces of tyre on securely.

**12.** Finally tape the pieces of foam to the wood on the opposite side to the straps.

**13.** When you are wearing the stilts the wooden post will run up the outside of your leg with the straps on the outside and the foam on the inside.

### Useful Tips

Your local resource centre, junk or charity shops may provide some of the materials free or at minimal cost.

Ask your local bicycle shop for any old tyres that they are throwing away.

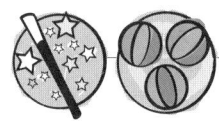

— CAN DO —

## Safety Check

Be extra careful when using tools and ensure that you wear protective glasses at all times.

The use of tools should always be taught and supervised by someone with skills and experience in using them.

It is particularly important that all of your drilling and sawing is accurate to ensure that your stilts will fit together well and be safe to use.

Always ensure that the nuts and bolts are tight and you strap yourself in well before using your stilts.

Make sure all tools are stored correctly and in a safe place

## What next?

Learn to use your stilts safely - see Stilt Walking on page 73.

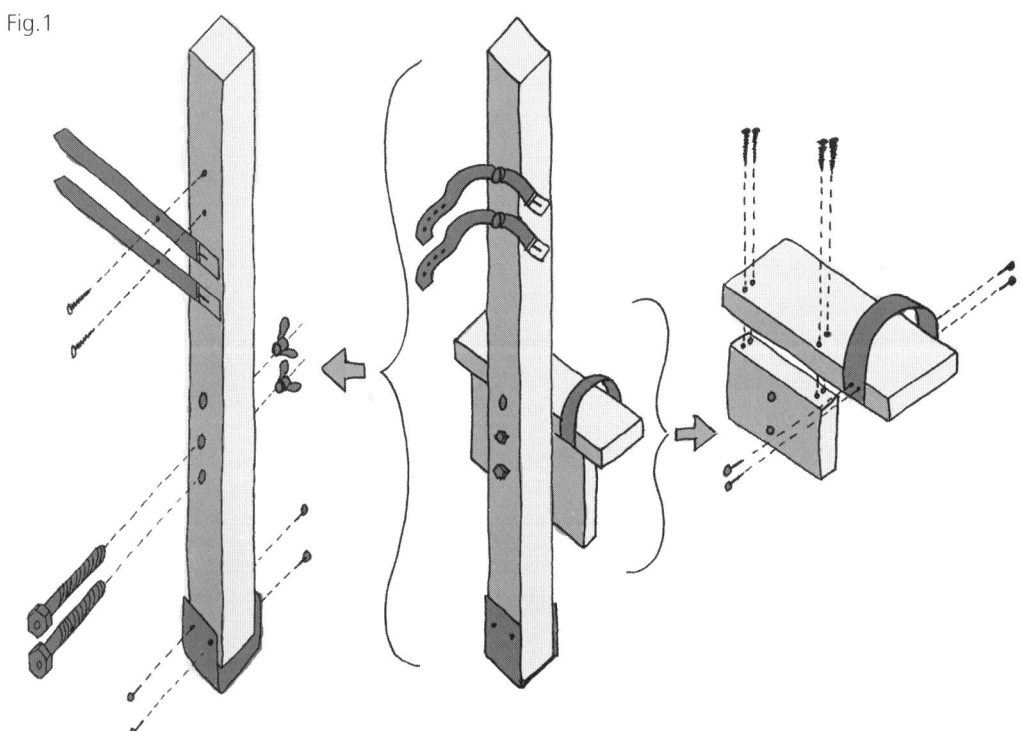

Fig.1

COOL CREATIONS

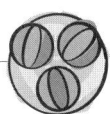

# Stilt Walking

## Why we like it

Stilt walking has been around for centuries and its still as much fun to learn as ever. From village fetes to the big top stilt walkers the world over have wowed audiences of all ages. Learning to walk on stilts improves balance and co-ordination and can be a great confidence booster. It is also a great skill to be able to contribute into a performance, show or festival.

## What you might need

Stilts—either bought or home made
Chairs.

## How many can do it

Depending on equipment available and the level of those using it there is no limit to the number of people who can participate. When starting out it is useful to work in pairs with one guide on the ground and the other following on stilts.

## Where can you do it

Inside or outside so long as it is dry and you are on a smooth flat surface. You will need an area with at least one wall to lean on and some chairs to start off from and to finish on. Gyms and halls are good as they generally have supports on the walls that can be very useful.

## Useful Tips

Look directly in front of you when walking and not at your stilts—this will improve your ability to balance and avoid walking into obstacles.

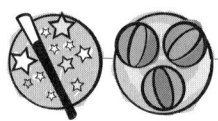

CAN DO

## How you can do it

1. Work with a partner taking turns to use the stilts yourself and then to guide your partner. Attach the foot platform to the lowest setting and tighten the fixing nuts and bolts. Check the rest of the fixings on the stilts to ensure that all are firm and the stilts are safe to use.

2. Whilst seated push your toes into the toe strap ensuring that the whole of your foot is firmly on the foot platform. Cover your lower leg with the foam section and tighten the straps around the lower part of your leg, make sure the straps are firm but not too tight.

3. Get your partner to help you stand so that you can hold onto them and onto a wall.

4. Take very small steps from one foot to another to get a feel for your balance on stilts.

5. When you feel more confident and whilst holding onto your partner and the wall begin to take slightly larger steps—stay in control and feel for your balance on the stilts.

6. When you feel confident enough, ask your partner to lead you slightly away from the wall, and try to take a few steps between your partner and the wall unaided. Increase the distance until you feel confident to walk unassisted.

7. Once you have mastered your balance on stilts you can try raising the level of the foot platform for a 'taller' view of the world.

### What next?

Show Off! Offer your services as a stilt walker to others planning shows or events or put on a performance yourselves.

#### Stilt Walking Costumes

You can add some colour by painting your stilts to your own design. Why not add feet to your stilts by nailing a pair of old shoes to the bottom of each stilt—remember to cut a hole for the stilt to go through and nail the shoe to the outside of the stilt, not the bottom.

Make some stilt walker's trousers—make a large pair of long, baggy trousers that cover your legs. Add the shoes to the bottom of the stilts for reality and nobody will know the difference.

## Safety Check

The higher you are off the ground the more potentially dangerous this activity is - you may want to wear protective pads - knees and elbows and a helmet.

## Spotlight

Having someone to hold onto in the early stages of learning can be a great help and once you have mastered the basics you can help others to pick it up by leading them around on their stilts whilst on yours. Working in this way can encourage the development of co-operation and trust.
Working in pairs or groups can help all involved to learn more quickly.

COOL CREATIONS

 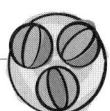

## The Final Curtain—Putting on a Circus Show

### Why we like it

Putting on a circus show or display can be a great way to bring together work on a number of projects and to give a platform for your newly acquired skills. You can use all sorts of elements from juggling and stilt walking to tumbling and Clowning. There is something for everyone to do from performing to working back stage to help others prepare. If you are a real extrovert why not run the show and introduce each act?

### What you might need

Equipment for performers—
stilts and juggling balls
Costumes
Performers
Ring master
Running order
Commentary.

### Safety Check

Make sure you are confident in the skills you will perform. Ensure there is enough space between you and the audience.

### How many can do it

You can put on a show single handed or gather others in your club to contribute. There is no limit to the number of people who can take part.

### Where can you do it

Inside or outside, but make sure you have enough space around you and that the ceiling height allows you to juggle. If it is windy you may need to change your juggling activities, plan ahead for these possibilities.

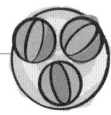

CAN DO

## How you can do it

1.  Decide on the sort of circus or show you would like to put on. Will it be just one person or many? Will it be inside or out? Will the audience be seated or will you put on the show around them while they are walking around at a fair or fun day?

2.  Decide on the number of acts or sections there will be to your show. Think about who may be best to present each element. You may want to hold auditions and ask those who audition for ideas for acts too.

3.  When planning the show think about how you will begin—how can you get the audience's attention? What is the best way to lead into the first act?

4.  Then think about the order of the acts for your show. Start with the easiest elements and get the audience involved. Build up the excitement as the acts get more difficult.

5.  Save your best until last. Your last act should be the hardest and should be a fitting end to a fantastic performance. Build up the excitement and enthusiasm of the audience before you deliver your show-stopping party piece.

6.  Throughout your planning think about how you can include the audience. Will they hold some equipment, provide items that you will then juggle, have to shout a response at a particular moment or will they just bring the house down when a trick comes off?

7.  Rehearse. Make sure that all of the acts have practised their parts for the show and that they are confident. Then practise fitting all the acts together. How will you move from one act to another—will the ring master have a script or is there a way to get the two acts to hand over to each other?

8.  Publicise your show. Make sure that everyone knows about the show—where it is, what is on offer and when they need to be there.

9.  Get all the performers together to run through the show so that everyone is sure of their part.

10. Go For It!

## What next ?

Costumes can really add to a performance. Think about making your own costumes or finding costumes in a jumble sale or charity shop. Make sure that your costume offers enough room to move around in. You might want a theme for the whole performance that is carried through to the costumes - you could have a 60s or 80s costume theme with clothes from charity shops or make up your own costumes with animal print fabric and continue the jungle theme with the scenery and backdrop. Once your show is successful you can offer your services to others in the area by providing jugglers or stilt walkers for events or shows they may be running.

## Snapshot
### Building up the Tension

We found we had a real star in Gita. She built up the suspense by letting the audience know what was about to happen and just how difficult it was: 'for her next trick Jo will attempt the world famous single-stilt-stand, a trick rarely seen. If she makes this one, folks, we want a really big round of applause ... quiet in the audience please for this most difficult of manoeuvres.' This had the crowd on the edge of their seats and once the trick was performed they nearly literally bought the house down!